The Killing Fields of Inequality

The Killing Fields of Inequality

Göran Therborn

polity

The right of Göran Therborn to be identified as Author of this Work has been asserted in accordance with the UK Copyright, Designs and Patents Act 1988.

First published in 2013 by Polity Press
Reprinted 2014 (twice), 2015, 2016, 2017 (twice), 2019, 2020, 2021 (twice)

Polity Press
65 Bridge Street
Cambridge CB2 1UR, UK

Polity Press
350 Main Street
Malden, MA 02148, USA

ISBN-13: 978-0-7456-6258-9
ISBN-13: 978-0-7456-6259-6 (pb)

A catalogue record for this book is available from the British Library.

Typeset in 11 on 13 pt Sabon
by Toppan Best-set Premedia Limited
Printed and bound by CPI Group (UK) Ltd, Croydon, CR0 4YY

The publisher has used its best endeavours to ensure that the URLs for external websites referred to in this book are correct and active at the time of going to press. However, the publisher has no responsibility for the websites and can make no guarantee that a site will remain live or that the content is or will remain appropriate.

Every effort has been made to trace all copyright holders, but if any have been inadvertently overlooked the publisher will be pleased to include any necessary credits in any subsequent reprint or edition.

For further information on Polity, visit our website: www.politybooks.com

Contents

Figures

Tables

Introduction

Inequality is a violation of human dignity; it is a denial of the possibility for everybody's human capabilities to develop. It takes many forms, and it has many effects: premature death, ill-health, humiliation, subjection, discrimination, exclusion from knowledge or from mainstream social life, poverty, powerlessness, stress, insecurity, anxiety, lack of self-confidence and of pride in oneself, and exclusion from opportunities and life-chances. Inequality, then, is not just about the size of wallets. It is a socio-cultural order, which (for most of us) reduces our capabilities to function as human beings, our health, our self-respect, our sense of self, as well as our resources to act and participate in this world.

Outside philosophy, where, thanks to the late John Rawls, there has since the early 1970s been a significant interest in it, there has been little scholarly attention to inequality as a general plague on human societies. After Ricardo in the early nineteenth century, there was a long precipitous decline of economic interest in distribution, from which there is significant recovery in recent times, but – understandably – mainly, if not exclusively, concerned with inequality of income and wealth. The works of Anthony Atkinson, Branko Milanovic, Thomas Piketty and others have vastly widened our horizon of empirical knowledge.

Classical sociology had no focus on inequality, and in the American decades of post-World War II sociology, it took at least until the mid-1960s (Lenski 1966) before inequality became a mainstream concern. Even then, Gerhard Lenski's book on *Power and Privilege* is subtitled 'A Theory of Social Stratification'. In the earlier handbook literature (Lazarsfeld and Rosenberg 1955; Lipset and Smelser 1961) it is completely absent (true, the second deals with distribution of 'prestige'). Only from Smelser (1988) on is inequality officiously awarded a legitimate place in sociological investigations. Among the fifty-odd Research Committees of the International Sociological Association, there is no one focused on inequality. The nearest *Ersatz* is RC 28 on 'Social Stratification', a strange concept, imported from geology into sociology by a great, conservative Russian sociologist who emigrated to the US, Pitirim Sorokin (1927). In Sorokin's tradition, the Committee has mainly been interested in inter-generational social mobility, more popularly known as 'inequality of opportunity', a field in which impressive technical skills have been developed and deployed.[1]

More than a discipline, sociology is a vast field of many different pursuits, by different methods, so on most facets of inequality there is some sociological research. However, so far, there has been no attempt, in any social science discipline, to put a spotlight on the multidimensionality of inequality and its nefarious consequences. The general theoretical discussion has been

[1] A valuable insiders' self-appraisal of the Committee's achievements over fifty-five years is given by Hout and DiPrete (2006).

carried from philosophy to the social sciences by the economist Amartya Sen, and the broadest empirical discussion has been opened by epidemiologists – by Michael Marmot (2004) and Richard Wilkinson (1996, 2005; Wilkinson and Pickett 2009).

This abdication by sociology, the least bounded and the most generous of the social sciences, may now be ending. The International Sociological Association has decided to devote its next World Congress, in Yokohama in 2014, to inequality.

Citizens have been more impatient. In 2011 inequality was present, red-hot, in the streets: in the Mediterranean opposition to unequal austerity; in the Arab rebellions against unequal freedom and opportunity; in the Chilean student (and middle-class-supported) rejection of unequal higher education; in the Occupy movements of the US, the UK and other places, against the rule of the 1 per cent. Inequality even became a theme of the corporate Alpine leisure of the World Economic Forum at Davos.

This book's effort, which continues previous ones (e.g. Therborn 2006), has some distinctive features among the currently growing literature on inequality. It is resolutely multidimensional in its approach to inequality, focusing on health/mortality, on existential degrees of freedom, dignity and respect, as well as on resources of income, wealth, education and power. Secondly, it uses a historical global perspective, trying to grasp, comprehend and explain global as well as intranational developments over modern time. Thirdly, it tries to spell out the various mechanisms through which inequalities are produced. Fourthly, it pulls out mechanisms of equalization, and attempts to grasp historical moments, processes and policies of equalization. Increasing inequality is not inevitable. Finally, it offers an agenda for overcoming, or at least reducing, inequalities.

In-equality, as I shall elaborate somewhat below, is a normative concept, denoting the absence, the lack, of something – i.e., of equality. This normativity had better be recognized and reflected upon from the outset. But stated as a premise of concern, assessing its actual prevalence, identifying its causal mechanisms, and spelling out its social consequences are all procedures subject to possible scholarly falsification.

This book has two main aims: to convince students and academic colleagues of the necessity of a multi-dimensional and global approach to inequality; and, above all, to raise concern about existing multiple kinds of inequality, and to promote commitment to equalization among my fellow citizens of the world.

Ljungbyholm, Sweden
Göran Therborn
University of Cambridge

I

The Fields

You have probably heard and read quite a lot about inequality in these years of financial crisis, but how much have you discerned about kinds of inequality other than those of income and wealth? About inequalities of health, lifespan and death, for instance? About how the unequal life situations of parents are affecting the bodies and the minds of their children? And how much have you noticed about various processes of equalization currently going on in some parts of this world? What opportunities have you had to look under the cover of 'globalization', at how and to what extent the processes of distribution in different areas of the planet are interconnected and interacting? If you don't agree with the current state of inequality, what institutions have to be changed first of all? What social forces can you hope for, and join if you should want?

Theorization about inequality made great advances in the decades preceding the current economic crisis, above all in the disciplines of social philosophy and of medicine and epidemiology – advances which have not yet been absorbed into mainstream social science or into general public discourse. Crucial theoretical questions are still left unanswered, not seriously reflected upon. What is wrong with inequality? Why do we resent the economic inequality of some, and admire that of others – of sports and entertainment stars, for example? What is the difference between inequality and difference? What kind of equality should contemporary democratic and libertarian egalitarians strive for? What are the social mechanisms through which inequality – and equality – are produced?

The question marks above, and other, related ones, have motivated me to add this contribution to the ongoing debate. While paying due attention to Mammon and his devotees – as well as my respect to his economic analysts – I am arguing that the violations of human capabilities which inequality constitutes require a much broader empirical and a much deeper theoretical approach than the existing offers.

Let us begin by looking at the fields of current experience.

1

Human, Nasty and Short: Life under Inequality

The Short Lives of the Unequalized

Inequality kills. Between 1990 and 2008, life expectancy for White American men without a college degree fell by three years, and White low-educated women had their lives shortened by more than five years (Olshansky et al. 2012: exhibit 2). Only AIDS in southern Africa and the restoration of capitalism in Russia have had a more lethal impact than the US social polarization in the boom years of Clinton and Bush. African Americans have shorter lives than White Americans, but here the gap has actually narrowed in the last two decades – after an early twentieth-century widening – between 1990 and 2009 (*National Vital Statistics Reports* 60:3, 2011, table 8). Inequalities of race and education together – Blacks with less than twelve years of education vs Whites with more than sixteen – cut the lives of the disadvantaged by twelve years in 2008 (Olshansky et al. 2012: 1805). That is the same as the national difference between the USA and Bolivia (UNICEF 2012: table 1).

The return of capitalism to the former Soviet Union meant a dramatic unequalization and mass impoverishment. In Russia, the Gini coefficient[2] of income inequality was hoisted from 27 in 1990 to 46 in 1993, in the Ukraine from 25 in 1992 to 41 in 1996 – then continuing to rise, to 52 and 46 in 2001, respectively (UNICEF 2004: 117, 123). By 1995 the restoration processes had generated 2.6 million extra deaths in Russia and the Ukraine alone (Cornia and Paniccià 2000: 5). For the 1990s and the whole of the former USSR, the death toll amounted to 4 million, according to the British epidemiologist Sir Michael Marmot (2004: 196; cf. Stuckler et al. 2009).

After a catch-up in the 1950s and early 1960s, the health situation in the Soviet Union and Eastern Europe had stagnated, even deteriorating in some countries, including Russia. But the restoration of capitalism meant a sudden jump in mortality, with the standardized death rate among Russian men (aged 16 and over) increasing by 49 per cent between 1988–9 and 1993–4, and among Russian women by 24 per cent (Shkolnikov and Cornia 2000: 267).

The Marmot estimate of 4 million excess deaths in the 1990s is considerably lower than the mortal effects of the Stalinist collectivization of the 1930s, of which the best estimate for the 1927–36 period seems to be *circa* 9 million (Livi-Bacci 1993: 751ff., 2000: 50), with a particularly devastating impact in Kazakhstan and Ukraine (Ó Gráda 2009: 237). However, with respect to Russia, the collectivization tragedy of the 1930s and the privatization one of the 1990s are not incomparable.

---

[2] Named after an early twentieth-century Italian statistician, the coefficient is the most frequent measure of income distributions. It runs from zero, for full equality, to 1 – or to 100 in multiplied form – when one party takes everything. In contemporary societies it varies between 0.2 (or 20), in some Nordic and East-Central European countries of the 1980s, to 0.75 (or 75), counted in some African cities, like Johannesburg, around 2000.

From 1930–1 to 1933 the (crude) Russian death rate increased by 49.5 per cent (Livi-Bacci 1993: 757), i.e., almost exactly the same increase as sixty years later. Russian and Ukrainian extra deaths in the 1990s, through mass unemployment, mass impoverishment and degradations, may well be argued to have been less brutal than those from the requisitions, famine and deportations of the Stalinist collectivization. But the silent acceptance of new systemic deaths by the world's liberals and conservatives is more amazing in the mediatic, 'information age' 1990s, than the starry-eyed disbelief among the Communists and Soviet admirers of the insulated 1930s.

By 2009, life expectancy in Russia and the Ukraine is still below what it was in 1990 (WHO 2012: part III, table 1). The educational gap in life length widened in Russia while death rates rose in all educational groups (Shkolnikov and Cornia 2000: 267). But in Estonia and Lithuania in the 1990s, a dramatic increase in dying among people with, at most, upper secondary education accompanied a mortality decline among the highly educated (Leinsalu et al. 2009).

The main Western European pattern of unequal life possibilities is a stagnation or a slow lengthening of the lifespan of the poor and the low-educated, while the life horizon of the rest is being extended. This seems to be the trend of the last half-century or more (Valkonen 1998) – in the UK, roughly since the introduction of the National Health Service (no causal connection implied) (Fitzpatrick and Chandola 2000: table 3.8). After a spike in the mid-1990s, the English gap between occupational classes I and V has decreased somewhat, while differences in life prospects between territorial areas have continued to grow, and the inequality coefficient of age at death has risen (Sassi 2009). Just between 2004–6 and 2009–10, the lifespan gap between Glasgow and Kensington–Chelsea increased by more than a year (Office of National Statistics 2011). The American pattern is similar, but includes a growing mortality gap, in relation to the richest quartile of the population, in the second and the third quartiles as well (Evans et al. 2012: 15).

Some recent changes elsewhere in Western Europe are rather dramatic too. For example in Finland, the life expectancy gap at the age of 35, between the richest and the poorest fifth (quintile) of the population, widened by 5 years for men and 3 years for women in the period from 1988 to 2007. It is now 12.5 years between the top and the bottom male quintile, and 6.8 between the female ones (Tarkiainen et al. 2011). Another Finnish study by the same group of researchers found that the (age-standardized) death rate at ages 35–64 among the poorest fifth of women increased strongly from 2004 to 2007, leaving it well above the level of the late 1980s. Premature deaths among the unemployed and among people living alone also soared between 1988 and 2007, among both men and women (Tarkiainen et al. 2012: tables 1–2).

A number of large longitudinal studies have established that unemployment produces extra deaths, even when controlling for stress palliatives like tobacco and alcohol, as well as for pre-unemployment health (e.g. Bethune 1997; Gerdtham and Johannesson 2003; Moser et al. 1994; Nylén et al. 2001). Even the wives of unemployed men have been found pushed into the grave before other married women (Moser et al. 1994). One of the direst consequences of the ongoing financial crisis is its generation of mass unemployment. The megalomania of a few hundred recklessly gambling bankers has thrust millions of workers into unemployment. From early 2008 to January 2013, the unemployed in the EU increased by 8 million, to 26 million, and in the USA by 4.6 million to 13 million. How many of these unemployed will die a premature death? We don't know yet, but they are likely to be numbered in tens of thousands.

At the International Court in The Hague, people are convicted of 'crimes against humanity' with smaller mortal dimensions.

Level of education is in some sense the sharpest and most comparable instrument for measuring social inequality of premature adult death. It doesn't in itself explain mortality, although it does indicate life-long effects of childhood and youth experiences – we shall return to this below – but it is relatively precise and internationally comparable, and it does point to something important: the early shaping of people's life-chances. It is often more powerful than income or wealth. For instance, in USA a college-educated White man at age 50 has 6 more years to live than a college drop-out. Wealth among the highest quintile gives a life premium of 4 years, full-time employment 3.4 years more than unemployment, and marriage a 2.5-year life advantage (Pijoan-Mas and Rios-Rull 2012). A recent European study of mortality also found (three-layered) education making larger differences than manual vs non-manual occupation. Self-assessed health, on the other hand, was more strongly differentiated by income, especially in England and Norway (Mackenbach et al. 2008: 2473, 2477).

Where is there most inequality of life and death in Europe? A Dutch research group at the Erasmus University provides an answer, referring to (standardized) rates of death between the ages of 30 and 74 in the 1990s. The answer is: East-Central Europe (Russia and the Ukraine were not included). Compared to people with tertiary education, every year 2,580 more people out of 100,000 with only primary education died before the age of 75 in Hungary, 2,539 in Lithuania, 2,349 in Estonia, 2,192 in Poland, and 2,130 in the Czech Republic. In (conventionally) Western Europe, Finland had the steepest slope of inequality: 1,255 annual extra deaths among the low-educated; France had 1,042,

Switzerland 1,012, and England-*cum*-Wales 862. Least lethal inequality was found in Sweden – 625 excess deaths – and areas in Spain (from 384 in the Basque country to 662 in Barcelona) and the Italian city of Turin (639). The above are male data, female deaths exhibit similar social and national patterns, but differentials are smaller, less than half the male average. In the women's league, the Nordic women come out relatively more unequal than the men. Swedish women are more unequal than French and Swiss women, and Norwegian and Danish women are even more unequal than the European average, whereas Finnish women, in contrast to Finnish men, are below the study's European average (Mackenbach et al 2008: table 2).

Not only death comes earlier to the poor and the little-educated. Common chronic diseases also start substantially earlier, if they arrive. An American study found various cardiovascular diseases, diabetes and chronic lung disease hitting people with eight years of education five to fifteen years earlier than people with at least sixteen years of schooling (Elo 2009: 557f.). A study of Finnish and Norwegian chances of living from 25 to 75 without any longstanding illness found that beside a higher risk of death, men with only basic education had seven to eight years more of longstanding illness (out of the fifty) than their compatriots with higher education. Low-educated women could count on a good extra five years of ill-health (Sihvonen 1998: table 3).

World inequality provides newborn children with very different prospects, not only of life-paths but of survival. Child and infant mortality is coming down, perhaps the most important developmental success in recent years. Nevertheless, in Africa in 2010 around 1 child in 9 (sub-Saharan average) died before the age of 5, and more than 1 in 6 in the worst areas of the world, such as Angola, Chad and Congo. In the safest parts of the rich world (Nordic countries, Japan, Singapore), this fate nowadays befalls 3 children in 1,000. The ratio between the best and the worst countries in terms of child survival until age 5 is currently 60:1.

Inside countries, there are, of course, vast differences in chances of child survival, according to mother's education, parental income or region. In Brazil in the 1990s you had a ten times better chance of surviving to your first birthday if you were born to a mother with twelve years of education rather than to an illiterate mother (Therborn 2011: 150). In Nigeria around the year 2000, about 200 more children in every 1,000 died before the age of 5 in the poorest fifth of the population than in the richest fifth. In several other African countries, and in Colombia and India, the differential was around 100 per 1,000. The Bangladeshi and Pakistani child mortality differential was about half the Indian one (data from 1996–2004, Houweling and Kunst 2009: figure 1).

The life-expectancy gap between the rich-country group and the least-developed countries was 27 years in 2010; between individual countries it reached 46 years: between Sierra Leone and Japan. Among the rich countries, it is notable that US life expectancy, at 78, is below the average rich-country level of 80, and a year lower than in Cuba (UNICEF 2012: table 1). The US infant mortality rate is above the OECD[3] average, and the rate in Washington DC is level with Romania's and

---

[3] The Organisation for Economic Co-operation and Development, an organization of the most developed countries of the world, based in Paris. For long consisting of Western Europe, North America, Japan and Oceania, it recently expanded to include also Chile and Mexico, and some Eastern European countries, like Poland and Hungary, as well as Israel and Turkey. It is important mainly as a producer of socioeconomic data and analyses, and for the diffusion of ideas, from market-oriented public management to childcare and labour market organization. Recently, it has devoted important efforts to analysing economic inequality, and to spreading an awareness of the issue.

higher than in Russia (Congressional Research Service, The US Infant Mortality Rate, figure 1, 2011, and UNICEF 2012: table 1).

The lethal force of inequality hits not only the poor and the little-educated. It also divides the affluent, the famous and the highest-educated. The British epidemiologist Richard Wilkinson (1996, 2005) launched in the 1990s a provocative hypothesis that (economic) inequality had negative effects on the lives and deaths also of people not at the bottom of the heap. His empirical argumentation and that of his followers was largely based on area studies, from rich countries to American neighbourhoods, which gave rise to fierce methodological battles. The controversy is not yet settled: the causal pathways remain too obscure and the ideological stakes are too big for that. But Wilkinson's hypothesis continues to find support, and in particular, perhaps, from a large-scale American study using individual data on relative deprivation of income – in comparison with other people in the same state, of the same age, education and race – and, on the other hand, individual probability of death and self-reported heath. In this way, Eibner and Evans (2005) found that relative deprivation reduces health and increases chances of death. (Relative deprivation is an individual measure, of A being worse off than B and C, while inequality is a group measure of ABC together: the more inequality, the more relative deprivation.)

Actors and actresses who win an Oscar live more than three years longer than nominees who did not win (Redelmeier and Singh 2001). Nobel Prize winners have on average longer lives than other scientists (Rablen and Oswald 2008), it was found in a very sophisticated study of Laureates in Chemistry and Physics in the first half of the twentieth century.

The empirical evidence is undisputable. Inequality kills. Status inequality shortens the lives of the unequalized even on the Parnassus of film and science. But psychosomatic mechanisms linking social status to health and longevity are still little explored and understood (cf. Wolfe et al. 2012).

Stunted Lives

Stunting is primarily an indicator of undernourishment of children. Technically, in international statistics it refers to children more than two standard deviations shorter than the median height for their age according to WHO standards. It is a condition with life-long consequences. Almost half of all Indian children under 5 are stunted, and almost 40 per cent of African children south of the Sahara, as well as of Indonesian children. About a third of Vietnamese children are affected, a quarter of South African, a sixth of Mexican, but only a tenth of Chinese and 7 per cent of Brazilian. The phenomenon is absent from the post-Communist European countries as well as from the rich world (UNICEF 2012: table 2). From what is known about child development in the rich countries (see, e.g., Milburn et al. 2009: 28ff.) – i.e., of life-enduring, even trans-generational, effects of childhood deprivations – this massive malnutrition must have a tremendous impact on human development in South and Southeast Asia and in Africa. Little seems to be known about it, however.

Stunted children are, of course, a product of intra-national as well inter-national inequality. In South and Southeast Asia, stunted children amount to almost 60 per cent of all in the poorest fifth of the population, but still a stunning 40 per cent among the richest – or rather the least poor – fifth. In sub-Saharan Africa, the same range is between *circa* 45 and 28 per cent stunted. A third of all Latin American children of the poorest 40 per cent of the population were stunted (Houweling and Kunst 2009: figure 4; data refer to 1990–2004).

In some parts of India, people are literally shrinking, in the midst of all the liberal middle-class hype and nationalist dreams of 'India Shining'. From the mid-1980s until the mid-2000s, the average height at age 20 declined for both men and women in the states of Delhi, Haryana and Punjab. In the big states of Uttar Pradesh (population 166 million in 2001), Bihar (83 million) and Madhya Pradesh (60 million), only women shrank, while men grew taller. In the states where both men and women grew in the last decades, men always grew better – in West Bengal and in Himachal Pradesh by about 1 centimetre per decade (Deaton 2008: table 2). It should be remembered that body height is a very important Indian criterion of beauty. I know of marriage matches which have run aground because the boy('s family) found the girl too short.

At least within some range of variation, body height is to a significant extent driven by the same biological processes as those driving brain growth. Taller children score better than shorter ones on cognitive tests from the age of 3, British and American studies have found (Case and Paxson 2008). There is also a positive correlation between childhood height and adult earnings, although part of that is probably generational class transmission of socioeconomic opportunities, from one better-nourished – in utero and after – upper-class kid to his/her offspring.

Lives are being stunted also by social malnutrition. Caste, misogyny and racism stunt the lives of 'Untouchables' and low castes, of girls and women, of stigmatized ethnic groups.

The life of *Dalits* has improved greatly under Indian independence. But it is only a generation ago that, as an 'Untouchable', you could not use the village store, temple or well, and economic exclusion is still a rule (cf. Sharma 1994; Thorat and Newman 2010). As a Black person in the United States, you could not check into an ordinary hotel or eat in an ordinary restaurant.

As a rural girl of northern India, or of the African Sahel, you still cannot expect to have any period of youth, having to move from a stern patriarchal childhood to getting married to someone ten years or more older, whom you don't know. Around 2000, more than half of rural South Asian girls were married off before their eighteenth birthday; in rural sub-Saharan Africa, almost half (UNICEF 2006: 48). In many African countries, decisions about a wife's health are taken by the husband alone – in Nigeria, 73 per cent of interviewed women reported this; in Bangladesh, 48 per cent; in Egypt, 41 per cent (UNICEF 2007: 18).

Your life may be systematically stunted for belonging to the wrong 'race' or ethnicity – for example, if you were non-White in apartheid South Africa or non-Jewish in today's Palestine, always subject to humiliating check-points, severe restrictions on travel, and repeatedly at risk of arbitrary incarceration and terroristic bombardments.

Even without casteism, racism and sexism, hundreds of millions have their lives stunted by dire poverty and chronic unemployment. The prospect of such stunting is what causes so many to put the only life they have at risk by trying to get illegally into the USA, Europe, Australia or the rich enclaves of Asia.

Children's lives are being stunted also in rich countries, and not by physiological undernourishment but by still unclear effects of parental inequality. Nationwide US surveys of the last decade show that the lower the income of their parents, the worse is the health of the children, whether measured in overall health assessment, limitations on activity, school absence for illness, emergency ward visits or hospital days. But there was no income gradient with respect to injury and poisoning or asthma. Parental income effects have been measured from the child's age of 2, and the differentials then grow with age (Evans et al. 2012: 5ff.). Life-long enduring effects of early childhood inequality have been shown by British studies following up life-courses of birth cohorts from the 1930s and 1940s, with impacts on income as well as on somatic and psychic health, and on life expectancy (ibid. 26f.).

In the 2013 obituaries of Margaret Thatcher, one of her important achievements was usually missing: a trebling of child poverty in the UK, from 7 per cent in 1979 to 24 per cent in 1992 (the poverty line is here defined as households with less than half of median household income, after housing costs). It was a lasting achievement – UK child poverty, although declining from the Blair government onwards, has never come near what it was before the Thatcher election. In 2010/11, it stood at 17 per cent, and its modest decline is projected to be reversed into increase until 2020 (Department for Work and Pensions 2012: table 4:1tr; Brewer et al. 2011).

A recent evil gift of Euro-American bankers is the effect of parental unemployment, from the burst financial bubbles, on the education of children. A recent Swedish study found a 'strong correlation' between adult unemployment and child school failure, stronger than the connection with immigrant background (*Dagens Nyheter* 26 March 2013, www.dn.se[4]).

Back in the 1970s, and into the 1980s in some countries, there was a movement for the 'humanization of work'. Included in this were socio-medical studies of work, stress and health. One of the most significant findings of these was the crucial importance of demand

---

[4] Unless otherwise indicated, all URLs cited were last accessed on 26 March 2013.

and control. High demands on your work – speed, precision, constant attention or strenuous effort – with little or no control of your work situation were likely to wear heavily on your health, somatically as well as psychologically (Karasek and Theorell 1990). Low rewards for big efforts were also likely to affect you badly. The conclusion of the humanization movement was to call for more workers' control and workplace influence, ideas now, under the aegis of employee 'flexibility' and 'employability', as distant as socialism – except in the creative IT industry.

The sense of lack of control over the process of systemic change and lack of approval of the new economic regime being installed experienced by most Russians seem to have been among the causes of the leap in self-assessed ill-health and in mortality there (Marmot and Bobak 2000: 130, 139–40).

These stressors of demands and control from above are institutionalized in hierarchies. They explain the remarkable findings of a large longitudinal study of the Whitehall central bureaucracy, from the porters and messengers to the permanent secretaries. Mortality, before retirement age, formed the same ladder as the bureaucracy, even after taking smoking and other risk factors into account: those at the bottom died first, those at the top, last (or rather, they had a greater chance of surviving into old age – Marmot 2004: ch. 2 and *passim*).

The portrayal of inequality as only a picture of the 1 richest per cent vs the rest is closer to the Disney world of Scrooge McDuck than to the grim realities of human life under contemporary inequalities.

2

Behind the Doors of Exclusion

Now that, in the wake of the financial crisis, there is a mainstream concern, even occasional outrage, at exorbitant executive pay and bonuses, a serious, independent-minded egalitarian should ask him/herself what, if anything, is wrong with huge differences of income and wealth? Is the mainstream, falling prey to envy (a feeling usually perceived as closer to vice than to virtue)? And how is the sudden outrage at executive pay related to the absence of any similar outcry against the vast sums raked in by the stars of sports and entertainment, generally venerated by the popular media – by the sports pages, in particular?

Mainstream 'common sense' should not be dismissed in the manner typical of the arrogance of privilege. Without trying to read the mainstream mind, we can see one obvious difference between celebrities, on the one hand, and bankers and executives on the other. The former give their public something. The celebrities appear as harmless butterflies, whose indulgent lifestyle provides vicarious enjoyment to their fans. But the captains of finance and of the rest of the economy are not entertaining us. They are ruling us.

The celebrity butterflies are also rather few. Among the US top one-thousandth (0.1 per cent) of income appropriators, they make up 3 per cent. Non-financial business executives made up 41 per cent in 2004, and financial executives and managers 18 per cent (Hacker and Pierson 2010: 46).

Inequality always means excluding some people from something. When it doesn't literally kill people or stunt their lives, inequality means exclusion: excluding people from possibilities produced by human development. There are two main doors of exclusion in human societies. One is slammed in the faces of the poor, a condition which takes on different shapes – say, in the UK and in India – but which has a universal social meaning. To be poor means that you do not have sufficient resources to participate (fully) in the everyday life of the bulk of your fellow citizens.

The other door of exclusion closes off the elite from the rest of the people. In capitalist regimes, that is the 0.1, the 1 or, at most, 5 richest per cent from the rest. In dictatorships based on state power, the 'elite' may be a tiny 'inner circle' around the dictator, or the top echelon of a hierarchical organization, as in Communist party-states. In both cases, this second door creates a divide between the commanders and the commanded, between the policy-makers and the policy-takers. The larger the gap between the 1 and the 99 per cent, the thicker the door of exclusion, the more distorted human cooperation and interdependence become, in favour of the former.

The main issue of economic inequality lies in its effects of social sundering, economic squandering, and political distortion and dictat-ship. The inequality of resources tears societies apart, into what Benjamin Disraeli (as a novelist rather than as a politician) once called 'the two nations': the rich and the poor. Thereby the social space for human development is carved up and restricted, above all for the disadvantaged, of course, but not only for them. Secondly, the inequality of ownership of, control of or access to economic resources means that what has been produced in a given society can easily be dissipated by the privileged few. Thirdly, inequality of economic resources and their political deployment has negated the nineteenth-century liberal fears of democracy: that citizens' power would encroach upon private property. Instead, big property owners have, most of the time in most countries, been able to dictate what is 'sound economic policy'.

Sundering

Resource inequality tears people apart. A dramatic outcry about it arose in the USA in 2012, in Charles Murray's book *Coming Apart*: 'Our nation is coming apart at the seams – not the ethnic seams, but the seams of class' (Murray 2012: 269). This very original, extremely interesting and best-selling book is significant also for adding a new perspective on inequality. Its author is a conservative writer and independent scholar, not known as an egalitarian – rather, the opposite. In a communitarian vein, Murray is concerned with the cultural rift and segregation in American society, primarily between, on the one hand, the college-educated managerial and professional class, and, on the other, the blue-collar class with – at most – a high-school diploma. Murray shows how the gap between the two has widened and deepened to a chasm since the early 1960s, and in order to highlight his class analysis he has concentrated mainly on the White classes. His principal empirical fields are marriage and family, work and labour force participation, crime, social and civic engagement, and religion – all fields in which the two classes have come asunder, becoming worlds apart.

In our context, it is Murray's descriptions which are relevant, sharp-focused, well documented. That he is weak on explanation and solutions need not concern us here. As a conservative moralist, Murray tends to substitute moral blame for social explanation, portraying the development as an effect of the secular counterculture of the 1960s, the moral degeneration of the poor, and the fact that the hardworking moral upper class does not preach what it practises. After a standard right-wing American dismissal of the European welfare states, Murray puts his hope on a new religious 'awakening'.

Still, for all his strident ideology, Charles Murray's graphic description of America cut apart by class is the most vivid current picture available of the socially sundering effects of resource inequality.

Another telling manifestation is the polarization of cities which took off in the last two decades of the previous century. On the one hand is the ballooning of closed private neighbourhoods, even entire cities like Alphaville in São Paolo or Nordelta on the outskirts of Buenos Aires, so-called 'gated communities' (cf. Paquot 2009). Often they are not much of a 'community', but they are privileged compounds shut off from the plebs. The concept developed in western USA, but the practice is now widespread outside the still relatively egalitarian areas of West-Central Europe and Northeast Asia. My personal experience is of a massive extension of such closed-off urban areas, in places like Manila, Bogotá, Mexico, São Paolo and, from the *années folles* of the 1990s, neoliberal Buenos Aires. What they amount to is a kind of social apartheid.

On the other hand is the production of what Loïc Wacquant (2008) has called 'advanced marginality', dumps of 'urban outcasts', succeeding and replacing the mid-twentieth-century American Black ghettos and

European working-class neighbourhoods, that were disadvantaged in many ways but home to employed industrial workers – in the American ghettos often with an ethnic middle class as well – and had their own collective culture: in the US, the multifaceted Black 'soul' culture, and, in Europe, the rich labour-movement community culture. A similar process got under way in the working-class suburbs of Buenos Aires in the 1990s and into the crash of the neoliberal experiment in 2001–3.

This extreme polarization is not the only big city game around. There are also heroic attempts at revitalization of declining, even shrinking, industrial cities, but again and again these attempts find themselves producing little more than new enclaves of privilege amidst continuing social dissolution, driven by contemporary financial capitalism's relentless inegalitarian driving of distanciation and exclusion.

Furthermore, as the world is getting an urban majority for the first time in human history, cities have become concentrations of inequality. Income inequality among the residents of the major South African cities, headed by Johannesburg, has a Gini coefficient value of 75 (UN Habitat 2008: 72), which is somewhat above the estimated inequality among all households on the planet: about 70 in 2008 (Milanovic 2012: 8). Many big cities are more unequal than their countries, like Johannesburg and Tshwane in South Africa, Brasilia, Mexico City, Buenos Aires, New York and Washington DC (and several other US cities). This is not the pattern in Europe generally, or in Tokyo, where cities come close to the national pattern. And, according to the UN Habitat, inequality in Beijing is only half that of the nation as a whole (UN Habitat 2008: 63ff.).

There is also what we may call the Marie Antoinette effect of incomprehension. According to French revolutionary tradition (perhaps apocryphal), Queen Marie

Antoinette, upon hearing that the people of Paris were demanding bread, asked her courtiers: 'Why don't they eat cake?'

A good illustration of the Marie Antoinette effect is recent (November 2012) legislation introduced by Sweden's bourgeois government. Sweden has been falling behind in the recent PISA[5] studies of school performance, because the lower stratum of Swedish pupils is performing worse than before. The response of the Swedish upper-middle-class government has been to introduce a tax rebate for parents who hire someone to help their children do their homework. So, the Marie Antoinette advice to the unemployed natives and the largely immigrant cleaners and paramedical assistants, whose children have difficulties with the current 'entrepreneurial' teaching and private–public school divisions is: 'Hire a homework helper, and fill in the forms to get a tax reduction.' An extra advantage of this policy of subsidizing middle-class educational privilege is that subsidized homework assistance is becoming a lucrative business, employing university students. Not only is overall middle-class educational privilege bolstered, a section of the same class is profiting from taxpayers' money.

And the more the rich differ from the rest of us, the harsher, the more inconsiderate their rule of us can be expected to be. In the latest US election, you heard the candidate of capital, speaking to his country-club peers, promising them he had nothing to offer the bottom 47 per cent of the population.

As Alexis de Tocqueville (1856/1966, esp. ch. 8) pointed out, almost two centuries ago, as a liberal aristocrat reflecting upon the anti-aristocratic French

---

[5] Programme for International Student Assessment, a recurrent comparative evaluation of the educational competence of 15-year-olds, initiated by the OECD in 1997.

Revolution, privileged social apartheid is a social practice, prone to spawn an 'indomitable hatred of inequality', and rebellion and revolution. It is certainly no path to stable and efficient social governance.

One very well-documented effect of tearing social webs apart is the sowing of distrust and fear, no assets of social development. Social science has firmly established that inequality breeds distrust (Uslaner 2002; Rothstein and Uslaner 2005). The correlation is not quite as neat as the fully parallel ladders of office hierarchy and premature death in Whitehall (ch. 1 above), but international differences in beliefs that 'most people can be trusted' are both large and strongly correlated with measures of income inequality. In Scandinavia, two-thirds of the population think that 'most people can be trusted'; in Brazil, 3 per cent; in South Africa, 12 per cent; in Britain, 30 per cent; and in the US, 36 per cent (Inglehart and Norris 2004: table A165).

Distrust and fear of others are a social cost. Necessary cooperation then requires extra safeguards. More resources have to be spent on security measures and bodyguards. An estimated tenth of the economically active population of Bogotá, capital of one of the most unequal countries in the world, are in the security/surveillance business.

However, an analyst – as opposed to a preacher – should point out that current rich capitalist societies need less cooperation than in the past, a process sustaining ongoing social sundering.

Less national cooperation is now needed. Mercenary armies have returned from the era of royal absolutism, replacing the citizens' conscription armies of the classical modern nation-states. Collective civic organizations can be and are now being overwhelmed by mass media blasts, professional NGO cadres and momentary Facebook campaigns. Neighbourhood solidarity is needed

Table 1   *Murder regions of the world. Homicides per 100,000 population,* circa *2010*

Southern Africa	30.5
Central America	28.5
Eastern Africa	21.9
Middle Africa	20.8
South America	20.0
The Caribbean	16.9
Western Africa	15.4
. . .	
Eastern Europe	6.4
. . .	
Northern America	3.9
. . .	
Eastern Asia	1.3
Western Europe	1.0
World	6.9

Source: UN Office on Drugs and Crime, www.undoc.org

less in the face of professional social assistance and social work interventions.

But disasters will strike, and reveal the fragility or the resilience of collective social organization, as in New Orleans in 2005 and in New York / New Jersey in 2012, respectively, or in every hurricane season in the different damage effect in Haiti and in Cuba. Urban and plane-tary environmental challenges are increasing the need for social collaboration.

Social sundering also means social violence. The world's most murderous areas are the most unequal regions (table 1).

Among larger countries, the most murderous were: South Africa with 32 murders per 100,000 population, Mexico with 23, Brazil 21, Nigeria 12, Russia 10. The USA had 4.8, India 3.4, the UK 1.2, China 1.0 and Japan 0.4. Behind the frequency of lethal violence we should expect complex causal configurations, including, *inter alia*, the importance of the drug trade, the strength and patterning of organized crime, traditions of social control, effectiveness of states. Social sundering by economic inequality is one major factor in these constellations.

Squandering

For us, the late-born, some of the examples of the most exorbitant squandering have become, millennia or a half-millennium later, aesthetic or even touristic experiences, like the terracotta army and the underground tomb city at Chang'an, the pyramids at Giza, the Taj Mahal at Agra – all monuments to death. However, the 2000s financial 'masters of the universe', for all their self-indulgent profligacy, seem to have left nothing of likely interest to the archaeologists and the tourists of the 2500s.

Squandering of economic resources, foreclosing their productive use, is something well known from horror stories about the world of 'development', for example from Marshal Mobutu's Zaïre, Emperor Bokassa's Central African Empire – eagerly courted by the American and the French political leaders, respectively – and from less flamboyant but no less devastating squandering in many rent-based political economies: Nigeria, Angola, Equatorial Guinea and others, including post-Communist Russia and its oligarchs. Idiosyncratic squandering on pet and prestige projects, and concomitant under-investment in infrastructure, education and productive capacity, are constant risks in highly unequal societies – in terms of power as well as of economic inequality.

But inequalities differ. The Gulf shaikhs have assumed a certain aristocratic norm of *richesse oblige*, and many

American moguls, from the Rockefellers to Bill Gates, have embarked on generous philanthropic endeavours, usually after ruthless practices of accumulation. Nevertheless, the blockage of the Obama administration's original plans to try to catch up with Chinese infrastructure and with European non-elite education, at the same time as expanding wars and military spending with the full support of the politico-economic elite, shows that the difference between American inequality and, say, Nigerian or Russian is only one of imprecise degree. In comparison with the Pentagon's annual $4.7 billion spending on public relations, staffed by 27,000 people,[6] Emperor Bokassa's coronation in 1977 was a cheap one-off event, for 20 million 1970s dollars.

In the recent period, the US, and UK-supported, wars in Iraq and Afghanistan amount to a gigantic squandering of public resources by a ruthless, privileged elite. Both wars were wars 'of choice', as their more intelligent protagonists pointed out, like *New York Times* columnist Thomas Friedman campaigning for the Iraq war, and Barack Obama for escalating the war in Afghanistan. The elites can afford these wars of choice, paid for by public money or public debt, vastly benefiting friendly business contractors, and not risking any elite lives. How much these ruling choices have cost is not yet clear, and the Afghan war with its Pakistani extension is not yet finished. But by the end of 2012, US costs amount to about $3 trillion, including interest on war appropriations and social costs to military families, but excluding long-term disability costs – of wounded Americans only, of course – estimated at more than $900 billion (www.costofwar.org). Together this is equivalent to the medium-term deficit reduction goal of $4 trillion set up by the 2010 National Commission on

[6] Hastings (2012), here quoted from the *New York Review of Books*, 27 September 2012, p. 61.

Fiscal Responsibility and Reform (the Bowles–Simpson Commission).

Alongside the American war spree, UK military squandering under Blair–Brown–Cameron has been more modest. By the end of 2011, British direct spending on military operations in its wars of (US) choice amounted to £28–9 billion (Berman 2012). But the ruling mentality in British politics is nicely conveyed by yet another one of its 'jolly little wars against barbarous peoples',[7] in Libya in the midst of sombre fiscal austerity – for the people – joyriding fighter planes at £35,000–72,000 an hour, and firing off missiles at £790,000–1,100,000 apiece. All costs of the dead, the wounded, and the disabled were, of course, on the bill of the natives.

Military squandering is no uniquely Anglo-Saxon pastime. The second biggest military spender (in relation to national income, after the USA) is Greece, even after the externally imposed austerity cuts, which largely spared the military (minus 5 per cent), concentrating on slashing pensions and civilian salaries (Dempsey 2013).

People's economic preferences differ. Quite rationally, poor people are more concerned about alleviation of poverty, jobs, income security, and public services and infrastructure than are rich people. Elites are interested in shielding their affluence from redistribution, and are usually more keen on projects of national splendour and prestige, and, in the case of actual or aspiring big powers, in international or world domination, with its requirements of displaying and deploying military might. Typically, the US Republican elite is crusading to cut all social rights and almost all kinds of civil spending, but

[7] The expression comes from a Tory politician with much more experience of it than David Cameron: Winston Churchill, referring to his own military training for imperial rule (Toye 2010: ch. 2).

appears rather to envisage a continuous increase in military and surveillance expenditure. The Cold War has turned into a seemingly unending series of small hot wars. In January 2013, David Cameron held out the promise of 'decades' of war against militant Muslims in Africa.

Nationalism and even enthusiasm for war are not alien to ordinary people, though. Thatcher's Falklands/ Malvinas war, for instance, had wide popular support. So had the hunt for Osama bin Laden. But the choices to invade Iraq in 2003, to extend the chasing of bin Laden out of Afghanistan into a thirteen-year war, with permanent partial occupation planned for after 2014, and the crushing of the Qaddafi regime in Libya had no popular roots, neither in the US/UK nor in the rest of NATOland.[8]

Given this normal preference scale for rich and poor, we have to expect that, other things being equal, the more the elite is unequal with the rest of the population, the more potentially common resources are squandered on pet projects of the elite.

---

[8] NATO (the North Atlantic Treaty Organization), set up in 1949 as an American anti-Communist military alliance, was never much concerned with democracy, including from the beginning authoritarian regimes like Portugal and Turkey. Only strong European resistance prevented the Americans from including Franco's Spain. After the end of the Cold War, the US decided not to disband NATO but to expand it, to anti-Russian Eastern Europe. Since then, NATO has been used as an international cover for US military interventions, in ex-Yugoslavia, Iraq, Afghanistan, Libya, etc. 'NATOland' refers to the US and its clientelist hinterland, in which the ex-imperial powers of Britain and France are trying to assert themselves. Through NATO, small countries, without any previous colonial glories, can now bask in the colonial sun over Iraq and Afghanistan. NATOland is now equivalent to a Colonial Club.

Political Dictat-Ship

A dictat-ship differs from a dictatorship. The latter may be seen as an extreme case of the former. In a dictat-ship there may be competitive elections and a diversity of media. A *Diktat* is an authoritative enunciation, a statement dictated to a secretary, or to any subservient body. It is a link between a powerholder and somebody having to take his dictamen or order. The crucial point here is that a political *Diktat* and a continuous series of them, a political dictat-ship, do not require a repressive dictatorship. The original manager–secretary dictamen only involved a pre-given power structure and compliance.

As a dissenter in a dictat-ship you don't run high risks of going to jail, unless you are suspected of 'supporting terrorism' – for instance by organizing support for the people of Gaza – but as a trade unionist or environmental activist in Latin America you might very well get killed, though not necessarily by the state. You may cast whatever vote you want, you may say whatever you like about the rulers of your country, but what you do and what you say have no, or little, effect, either in terms of impact or of landing you in jail.

In many countries, from Thailand to Nigeria, votes are extensively bought and sold. In the rich world, monetary electioneering is more subtle, but no less important. As a crucial election operative of both Clinton and Obama – currently Mayor of Chicago – Rahm Emmanuel, told his staffers, 'The first third of your campaign is money, money, money. The second third is money, money, and the press. And the last third is vote, press, and money.' Money six, votes 1 (Hacker and Pierson 2010: 252).

The *Diktat* turning democracies into dictat-ships comes from the top echelons of the inequality of money: 'Virtually all U.S. senators, and most of the representatives in the House, are members of the top 1 per cent when they arrive, are kept in office by the top 1 per cent, and know that if they serve the top 1 per cent well they will be rewarded by the top 1 per cent when they leave office' (Stiglitz 2011). Political scientist Larry Bartels (2008: ch. 9) has measured this dictat-ship in the US Senate. Neither Democratic nor Republican senators responded positively to any opinions from the lowest-earning third of their constituents. They were both moderately responsive to the middle third, and the Republicans were strongly responsive to the richest third of the voters.

Martin Gilens (2012) has taken Bartels'analysis and refined it further. The focus of his analysis is a comparison of a large number of answers to questions about policy preferences, in nationwide US polls of representative samples, with actual policy outcomes, mainly for 1981–2002, but with some extension to 1964–2006. One of his key findings is that, when income groups diverge in their preferences, the poorer half of the population has no chance of winning. Only the most affluent 30 per cent stand a chance, while the richest 10 per cent trump all others (p. 82). But he also finds that the influence of the richest 10 per cent varies with the policy domain – highest on economic and religious issues, lowest on social policy – and with the electoral cycle and the party constellation. Non-affluent voters have more influence close to an election and when the two parties are balanced in strength (pp. 101, 190). Without really going into it, Gilens also shows the importance of how the political system frames and processes the preferences of unequal citizens. For instance, in the mid-1960s, even a majority of the poor, it seems, 'opposed increased spending on aid to cities, on low-income housing, and on welfare and relief payments' (p. 222). Even citizen preferences can be dictated.

For the UK or from Europe generally I know of no similar studies. However, it is clear that the tone of British public discourse and British politics is set by a special social elite with an exclusive private education. In the current Conservative–Liberal Cabinet, 59 per cent come from an exclusive private education, as do 35 per cent of the current Members of Parliament. Perhaps even more noteworthy is that a third of the most recent Labour Cabinet also did, along with more than half of the country's top journalists (Milburn 2012: 3–4). In the UK, at least since Thatcher, it has been an axiom dictated by the upper and upper middle classes that taxation on income and property has to be kept down, or cut. In Germany and in the Eurozone, the prime non-negligible *Diktat* comes from the Bundesbank.

In Latin America until very recently, dictat-ships have alternated with dictatorships, the latter stepping in when the polity, say an elected president, does not heed the former. Land reform and income taxation have been held at bay by dictat-ship, and in the 'lead years' of the 1970s–1980s by dictatorship. The dictamina of business, transnational as well as national, are still keeping most of the unequal hemisphere on a very narrow path of redistributive capacity. In any capitalist democracy, the demands of a big capitalist have to be treated with more respect than a petition from 1,000 thousand citizens. That is the meaning of dictat-ship.

Many of us would concur with the cautious conclusion of Harvard philosopher Michael Sandel (2012: 203): 'Democracy does not require perfect equality, but it does require that citizens share in a common life.'

II

Theory

In the current flurry of public concern with inequality, very little theoretical reflection on the meanings and implications of inequality, and of equality, has come to the fore. While this small book is mainly a civic intervention sustained by empirical evidence, just to swim along with empiricist outrage would be a scholarly abdication, likely to facilitate a soon-to-come switch-off of the mainstream spotlights on inequality. A concern with inequality is a normative stance, entailing a vision of a good, rich human life. But the bases and the limits of its normativity have to be stated and motivated. As a social scientist, I am also under an obligation to spell out the basic processes and mechanisms of inequality and of equality.

Alas, my home discipline of sociology is not sufficient here, in spite of omnivorous empirical interests in inequalities and despite its disciplinary respect for pure theory. Windows have to be opened, in many directions.

3

Theoretical Cross-Draught

What we see is largely shaped by the frame of the glasses through which we look at the world. In order to grasp fully the issues of social inequality, to capture what is at stake, we need to open our conceptual windows, letting in fresh air from outside compartmentalized conventional discourses, academic as well as non-academic.

Here we shall weather four conceptual issues. What is the difference between a difference and an inequality? What equality is desirable to rational humans under the veil of ignorance of whether they would be advantaged or not under conditions of inequality? What is the relationship of poverty and inequality? Given prevailing presumptions, we should also raise the question: are there any analytical and ethical limitations to the liberal ideal of equality of opportunity?

The Difference between Difference and Inequality

Inequality, I hope to have shown above, is a major feature of today's world, and in many – if, as we shall see below, by no means all – respects it is increasing. But, after the discovery of Auschwitz and the end of apartheid, there is an almost universal belief in some kind of human equality, however immaterial. At the same time, we are probably more aware than ever that humans differ, having different shapes, gifts, values and experiences. Some clarification of the relationship between (in)equality and difference seems to be called for. Bluntly put, what is the difference between difference and inequality?

Difference and inequality were brought into confrontation by late Feminism. It questioned the social and economic concerns with gender inequality of the first cohort of 1960s Feminists. Instead, a new generation stressed differences between men and women, demanding space and respect for female difference. Difference, and the respect for it, soon became primary also to scholars and activists in the fields of ethnicity and migration.

- Differences are given (by God/nature) or chosen (styles), while inequalities are *socially constructed*.
- At the basis of inequality there is always some (assumed) *commonality*, which is exceptional and never necessary in perceptions/discourses of difference. Egalitarian Feminism assumed that there is a commonality between men and women, as human beings and as citizens. Difference Feminism bracketed commonality, as at most secondary.
- Inequality is a difference *violating* some *norm/* assumption of (this-worldly) equality (not necessarily explicit or clear), deriving from that commonality. Gender in-equality is a violation of a norm of human equality.
- Differences can and do coexist with equality as well as with inequality.

A remarkable, politically heavily loaded illustration of the difference between a difference and an inequality was brought up at the beginning of the French Revolution, resentfully referring back to an event at the last time the French General Estates had been summoned, in 1614. Then, the Third Estate (the commoners) had asked that the nobility should treat them as unequals: 'Treat us as your younger brothers, and we shall honour and love you.' In a letter to the King, the noble estate answered: 'Your Majesty, . . . Put them on to their duties, recognizing who we are, the difference that exists, and that they can in no way compare themselves to us.' In 1789 Sieyès, the leader of the Third Estate, wrote about this aristocratic stance as a target of the revolutionary demand for equality (Rosanvallon 2011: 28, my translation).

What Equality is Desirable?

The absence of equality may be found everywhere. But where and what is equality? Is it Nowhere; in Utopia? The politicians and the intellectuals of the French Revolution were grappling with the meaning of equality, to an extent hardly to be found in the United States, where none of the Founding Fathers seems to have seen any need for elucidating how slavery fitted into the Declaration of Independence's 'all men are created equal'. Indeed, George Washington could describe the last British Governor of Virginia as 'arch traitor to the rights of humanity' for having promised to free the slaves who went over to the British (Schama 2005: 18).

The French solution was to delimit equality to 'civic' or 'moral' equality, i.e., a secularized version of the Christian and Muslim notion of the equality of human souls. In his famous pamphlet *What is the Third Estate?*, Sieyès wrote: 'The inequalities of property and industry are like the inequalities of age, sex, and size etc. They do not distort [dénaturent] the equality of citizenship [civisme]' (Rosanvallon 2011: 74). That was a thin, liberal equality, which would not satisfy latter-day egalitarians.

On the other hand, few of us would be happy with radical nineteenth-century egalitarianism either, for instance with Gracchus Babeuf and his followers: 'Let there be no other difference between people than that of age or sex. Since all have the same needs and the same faculties, let them henceforth have the same education and the same diet.' I am citing from a book by Douglas Rae et al. (1981: 132) which is arguably the most incisive argument against simple, unreflective egalitarianism. Apart from the untenable thesis of sameness of needs and faculties in his quote from Babeuf, the strongest of Rae's five points against equality is that a crude egalitarian utopia would require that everything has to be allocated once and for all time. In empirical reality, the argument is somewhat less devastating. Pre-revolutionary Russian, post-revolutionary Chinese and traditional African villages have practised a redistribution of village land upon demographic family changes.

Marx was critical of this kind of one-size-fits-all equality, a view developed in his bad-tempered critique of the 1875 Gotha Programme of the unified German Workers' Party. An equal distribution of wages or goods is a right of inequality, Marx says, because individuals differ in performance and in needs. Equal distribution is a step forward from the inequalities of capitalist class society. But the banner of a future Communist society is different: from each according to his/her capacities (*Fähigkeiten*), to each according to his/her needs (Marx 1875/1969: 21). 'Needs' (*Bedürfnisse*) here is basically equivalent to what Amartya Sen a century later, with more precision, has called capability to function.

Ironically concomitant with the late twentieth-century turn to increasing economic inequality, egalitarian thought took a qualitative leap in sophistication, thinking hard and profoundly about the implications of diversity of needs and tastes, of freedom, of choice, and of responsibility for one's choices. This started off with John Rawls' *A Theory of Justice* (1971), which, through its sheer philosophical brilliance, spawned a whole generation of the highest-level social philosophy – although its utopian radicalism never had any political or ideological impact. This new stage of egalitarian philosophy has made some important inroads into economics, through Amartya Sen, who qualifies both as a philosopher and as an economist, but it seems to have attracted rather limited sociological interest.

For 21st-century practical – empirical–analytical as well as political – concerns about (in)equality, I think Sen's (1992: ch. 3, 2009: part three) definition of the equality we should strive for is the best: *equality of capability to function fully as a human being*. Such a capability clearly entails survival, health (and aids for disability), freedom and knowledge (education) to choose one's life-path, and resources to pursue it (cf. Nussbaum 2011). This might sound a bit abstract, but it has provided the theoretical inspiration and foundation for the UN *Human Development Reports* and their Human Development Index. I see the 'capability approach' as the best theoretical basis for analyses of and struggles against inequalities, which should be seen as multidimensional barriers to equal human capabilities of functioning in the world.

In this sense, *inequalities* are therefore *violations of human rights*, preventing billions of human beings from full human development.

While I am committed to equality as a value, I see no reason to spell out an ideal state of Equality. As Sen (2009: ch. 4) has argued with respect to justice, one

needs no 'transcendental' definition of the optimum to
be able to compare, to recognize whether inequality is
mounting or declining, or whether it is greater in the
UK than in, say, Germany. A focus on social bads, rather
than on a social ideal, was also a crucial decision of the
path-breaking, Swedish Social Democratic Level of
Living Investigations from the late 1960s, later exported
to several countries. And everywhere there is sufficient
inequality for us not to need to test the hypothesis that
this is the best of all possible worlds.

Inequality and Poverty

To some people, inequality may be of no concern, while
poverty is. The two can be conceptually separated.
Poverty may be a condition of (relative) equality, as in
China and Vietnam of the 1980s, and rising inequality
may be interpreted as part of a valley of transition from
poverty to affluence. But a poor population sector may
get stuck there, finding the route upward closed. In
developed, developing and underdeveloping countries,
in contrast to non-developed ones, poverty is a product
of inequality, of one or more of its four mechanisms (to
which we shall turn below).

To a large extent, your capability to function is
affected by the affluence or poverty of people around
you. Relative poverty is therefore a meaningful concept.
The severity of poverty also tends to depend on the
overall rate of poverty. Within the rich country club, the
OECD, the disposable income (at purchasing power
parities[9]) of the poorest tenth of the US population is

[9] Purchasing power parities are currency converters meant to
make income levels in different countries comparable in terms
of living standards. They are calculated on the basis of how

clearly below the thirty countries' average, while that of its top tenth hovers above the rest of the rich world. In terms of absolute deprivations, the American poor are worse off than the average European poor (west of the Balkans) with respect to 'constrained food choices', environmental conditions, arrears in paying utilities, rent and mortgages – and this was before the current crisis. The American poverty gap – the distance from the relative poverty line (of half the median household income) to the mean income of the poor as a percentage of half of the median country income – is higher than in any OECD country, save Mexico. The rates of relative poverty are highest in the three most unequal OECD countries: Mexico, Turkey and the USA. The UK is among the upper middle class of poverty and inequality, with more poverty and inequality than France, less poverty and more inequality than Germany, and much more of both than Scandinavia (OECD 2008: 37, 53, 127, 138, 154, 188).

Poverty is a trap easy to get stuck in, once you have fallen into it. In a selection of seventeen OECD countries, more than half of the people who had a disposable income less than half of the national median were still caught in poverty after three years. In the best welfare states, in the group represented by the Netherlands, Denmark and Germany, the share was 40 to 46 per cent. In the UK and in France half of the poor three years earlier were still poor; in the USA, 63 per cent (OECD 2008: 171).

much of a basket of commodities, say, 1,000 units of a country's currency can buy in that country in comparison with how much 1,000 dollars can buy in the USA. While better for this purpose than the official exchange rates, it is a difficult calculation prone to errors. In 2005 the World Bank made a major revision of its calculations.

Opportunity: Should 'Losers' Have Another Chance?

In conventional liberal discourse, much is made of a distinction between equality of opportunity and equality of outcome. The common-sense liberal is in favour of the former and more or less hostile to the latter. Two centuries ago, this was a radical idea, even revolutionary, and it remains a step of human progress from the *anciens régimes* of birthright. Since then, there has been considerable technical development of the concept. The American mathematical economist John Roemer (1998) has developed an algorithm for implementing equality of opportunity in welfare (be it life expectancy or lifetime income). World Bank economists Francisco Ferreira, François Bourguignon and others have taken Roemer's model further into empirical investigations. Looking into the empirical record, we shall return to such studies below. First we shall reflect a little on how far standard liberal egalitarianism would take us.

Most striking is its singular, pointilistic conception of social time. Opportunity is usually measured at one point in a person's lifetime: at birth, or early childhood, when gender, ethnicity, place of birth and father's (sometimes also mother's) education and occupation are measured. Students of occupational mobility normally look at two time points: at birth and at the age of maturing from school.

After birth, or at least after schooling, equal-opportunity individuals are on their own, solely dependent on their own effort, the outcome of which is their own responsibility alone. Is that all there is to human life? Suppose you are an Oxbridge graduate in classics, then you have a large set of labour market opportunities in front of you, although your chances of becoming Mayor of London may not be very big. Say you have a friend who is a graduate in (Arabic) classics from the University of Cairo. Her most likely opportunity is unemployment. How sure are you that she studied less hard than you? Or, assume that you chose a job in a big hierarchical corporation, but after some years you get a heart disease from the stress and the everyday put-downs of your superiors. Do you think that was because of your efforts? Another, hardly infrequent possibility: you may fall in love and have a child, maybe two even. Then love ends, and you are alone with two small kids, and you cannot climb the career ladder, perhaps not even keep your full-time job, because there is no affordable child care. Outcome: poverty. How much comfort would you get from your equality of opportunity?

To American conservatism, 'losers' should have no rights, no 'entitlements'. The Tea Party was launched by a television rant against any public support for the crisis 'losers' who could no longer pay their mortgages (Skocpol and Williamson 2012: 7). This is not the only conservatism conceivable, though. In the early 2000s, a successful American presidential candidate promised a 'compassionate conservatism',[10] and charity is an old conservative practice. The dismissal of outcome losers comes rather out of the liberal tradition and its overriding interest in opportunity.

Perfect equality of opportunity can also mean very different societies of outcome. Suppose we get liberal governments serious about equality of opportunity, and which succeed in making your lifetime income completely independent of your parents' resources, of your gender, your ethnic background and your place of birth. Your life's outcome depends entirely on your own choices, your drawing of education and labour market

---

[10] True, once elected, he soon traded compassion for bombing Iraq into 'shock and awe'.

Table 2   *Two societies of perfect equality of opportunity*
with different outcome structures

Society	Chances of getting into a group of earners	Group share of total income	Income per capita
A	1/100	20%	20
	9/100	20%	2.2
	70/100	58%	0.83
	20/100	2%	0.1
B	1/100	5%	5
	9/100	15%	1.67
	70/100	65%	0.93
	20/100	15%	0.75

lotteries, your preferences and your efforts. But the resulting society will be shaped by the parameters of your choices and efforts.

Let us take two examples, in both of which all individuals have exactly the same chances of lifetime earnings. Each of us has 1 per cent chance of winning, of getting one of the top incomes, getting into the One Per Cent of income receivers. Each of us has a 20 per cent chance of landing among the relatively poor, having to live on an income among the poorest fifth of the population; and we all have the same good chance of ending up in the middle. The only difference between our two example societies is their structure of income outcomes, embodied in different institutions and policy rules (table 2).

The numbers are fictive, as is the assumption of a serious liberal government of equal opportunity, but those of A are figures derived from Latin America *circa* 2000 and those of B from Scandinavia around 1980.

While societies A and B are both by definition perfectly egalitarian in terms of opportunity, their lifetime outcomes are very different. By purely individualist rational choice, 90 per cent of us would be better off choosing B rather than A, even without counting the better chances of trust, peace, and cooperation in society B.

Now, a diehard right-wing liberal might argue that this is a static picture. In a longer-time perspective, the more outcome-inegalitarian society A may generate more growth, and therefore, over time, more income even to the bottom 20 per cent, than B. This is a quite rational theoretical objection, but it belongs to the clouds of ideology, above social reality. Incentives do spur effort, but there is no empirical evidence supporting the argument that the more (outcome) inequality, the more growth. Currently, it seems that development economics is rather leaning to the opposite position. Anyway, long-term spectacular economic growth has been achieved both by low-inequality countries, like post-World War II Japan, South Korea and Taiwan, and through accelerating inequality, as in post-Maoist China.

In real social life, opportunities come and go, or pass by, all through your lifetime. Your set of probable opportunities at your moment of birth is more enduring and important, but you are facing one each day, dependent upon the outcome of yesterday. Inequality of opportunity at time 1 is significantly determined by inequality of outcome at time −1. The principled dichotomy between (in)equality of opportunity and (in)equality of outcome is a sociologically untenable ideological construction. If you believe in human rights, 'losers' have human rights too.

4

Three Kinds of (In)equality, and Their Production

Dimensions of Human Capability

The inequality which should bother all decent human beings is the unequal capability to function fully as a human being, the unequal capability to choose a life of dignity and well-being – under prevailing conditions of human technology and human knowledge. Although I am not here pursuing a philosophy of justice, again a question raised by Sen (2009: 414) turns out to be very helpful: what is it like to be a human being? What do you need to function fully as one? At least for analysing inequality, i.e., the denial of the capability of full human functioning, we had better concentrate on the hard core of Martha Nussbaum's (2011: 32) question: 'What does a life worthy of human dignity require?' *Pace* Nussbaum, this does not necessarily lead us to a list of 'central capabilities', but rather to the basic dimensions of human life.

Human beings are *organisms*, bodies and minds, susceptible to pain, suffering and death.

Human beings are *persons*, with selves, living their lives in social contexts of meaning and emotion.

Human beings are *actors*, capable of acting towards aims or goals.

From this we can derive three kinds of inequality.

1. *Vital inequality*, referring to socially constructed unequal life-chances of human organisms. This is being studied by assessing mortality rates, life expectancy, health expectancy (expected years of life without serious illness), and several other indicators of child health, like birth weight and body growth by a certain age. Surveys of hunger and malnutrition are also used.

2. *Existential inequality*, the unequal allocation of personhood, i.e., of autonomy, dignity, degrees of freedom, and of rights to respect and self-development. This was given a pregnant legal formulation in a British common law ruling in 1923 (on Canadian women): 'Women are persons in matters of pains and penalties, but are not persons in matters of rights and privileges' (Munroe n.d.).

3. *Resource inequality*, providing human actors with unequal resources to act. This is where most inequality discourse begins, with the arrival of the first pay cheque, disregarding the fact that by then many bodies have been buried, and many lives have been stunted for ever by humiliations and degradations. However, the central importance of resource inequality is undeniable. Resources of action are of several kinds, although following the money trail of income will take us quite far. As Michael Sandel (2012: 3) has pointed out recently, these days there are 'not many' things that money cannot buy. But your first resource is normally your parents, their wealth, their knowledge and their support. We shall pay our respect to them below, by looking into (in)equality of opportunity and social mobility.

Existential inequality is a concept which has not yet acquired recognized burgher rights in the social science community. There has also been a divide in social philosophy, around recognition versus redistribution, with Nancy Fraser valiantly defending the central importance of inequality and redistribution (Fraser and Honneth 2003). But several of its manifestations have already been and are being studied: women kept down and confined by patriarchy and sexism; colonized peoples by colonizers; the classes 'downstairs' by those upstairs; natives, immigrants and ethnic minorities ruled by *Herrenvölker* (master races); people with handicaps and disabilities or just the indigent overlorded by poorhouse wardens or condescending socio-medical powerholders; homosexuals pushed into closets by intolerant heteros; 'polluting' castes kept out of the way by higher castes, trampled-upon occupiers of the lower rungs of most hierarchies. Examples abound. And they all refer to unequal allocations of personal autonomy, recognition and respect, to denials of an existential equality of human persons, denied a capability of decent functioning.

This can be gauged and compared by looking into institutional norms, arrangements and discourse, into patterns of social interaction, the practices of powerholders and of keepers of expert knowledge, such as doctors; and, from the other side, by tapping personal experiences of restrictions and humiliations, through surveys as well as through qualitative interviews.

With regard to resource inequality, education is an increasingly potent aspect. While education is mostly studied in terms of access, Pierre Bourdieu (1979) made cultural inequality a distinctive focus of social analysis. So far virtually unexplored is the possible ideological trade-off between income and culture inequality, which can be seen on a broad spectrum of the American right. There, a generous magnanimousness towards income inequality and the rich goes together with an intense cultural resentment of 'overeducated elite snobs' (e.g. Murray 2012: 84).

Conventional studies of inequality concentrate on income, and no serious unconventional scholar should neglect conventions. So we shall pay ample attention to income inequality, *urbi et orbi*. Wealth is certainly an important resource, particularly in societies of land and mineral rent. But since most of today's super-rich are kept afloat by performance rewards, we shall here concentrate on income.

The social relations and the social contacts you can draw upon, whether to get a career recommendation, a loan, or for some comfort from distress, sorrow and loneliness, constitute an important resource, not just economically, politically and psychologically, but also for your somatic health. In this world of extreme capitalization, social relations are often called 'social capital', a term any scholar of human decency should avoid. Social connections or 'capital' are mostly used as an intermediary explanatory variable for other aspects of inequality, more seldom as a manifestation of inequality itself. While off-piste from our main argument, we have reasons to take social relations into account when looking at vital inequality.

Power is a potent resource for human action, arguably the main competitor to money. Inequality of power has so far only rarely been included in studies and analyses of social inequalities, and when 'political inequality' is addressed, it usually refers to inequalities of voting and of other forms of political participation. It should be taken more seriously, and related to different kinds of regimes, i.e., constellations of power. While not doing proper spatial justice to it, this study is bringing power into analyses of inequality.

The three dimensions interact and intertwine, and should always be suspected of doing so. But it should not be forgotten that they are irreducible to each other. Not only do they refer to distinct dimensions of human inequality; each has its own dynamic, and the dimensions do not always co-vary. For instance, in the rich countries, intra-national income inequality declined strongly from the end of World War I to *circa* 1980, while vital inequality – in the UK, which has the best data on this score – measured as the mortality rates of people aged 20–44 among different occupational classes, actually increased between 1910–12 and 1970–2 (Therborn 2006: table 1.12). Or take the place of Latin America in the world: while it is the most persistently unequal region of the world in terms of economic resources, there has for a long time been much less existential and vital inequality there than in, say, South Asia. The specific dynamics and the most important interactions between the three kinds of inequality may be laid out in the manner of table 3.

Population ecology here refers to environmental effects on the health, disease and death of human populations, such as the disease load of the tropics, and the lethal effects of early Euro-American urbanization, or of the polluted effects of contemporary slums.

Human status systems can take on many colourations, but the family–sex–gender system make up their core. Apart from their existential dimension, ethno-racial distinctions and relations also bear heavily upon resource inequality, and then back on existential hierarchy in a feedback loop. For instance, in Brazil, Guatemala and Peru, the most disadvantaged groups 'are composed exclusively of members of racial or ethnic minorities' (Ferreira and Gignoux 2011: 652).

Economic systems have most often been based on some intrinsic inequality, between those who own and those who work (only), and they have differed mainly in how the product of the latter is appropriated by the former. However, history has also known systems in

Table 3 *The roots, dynamics and interactions of the three kinds of inequality*

Kind of inequality	Roots & dynamics	Interactions
Vital	Population ecology Status system Medical knowledge	Sending: impact on Resource inequality Receiving: major impact from Existential & Resource inequality
Existential	Family–sex–gender system Ethno-racial relations Social status system	Sending: major impact on Vital & Resource inequality Receiving: major impact from Resource inequality
Resource	Economic, political & cognitive systems, ecology & performance	Sending: impact on Vital & Existential inequality Receiving: impact from Existential inequality, & from Vital inequality

which most of the economic players were equal individuals, gatherers, fishermen, hunters, farmers or socialist collectives. Throughout a large part of human history, politics has been based on tributes of the workers to the rulers. The past century of predominantly elected rule has created a new dynamics of (in)equality.

Livelihoods and economic systems are embedded in ecological space. More than half of income inequality in today's China derives from spatial location (Asian Development Bank 2012b: 70), and opportunity deprivation in two of the most unequal countries of the world, Brazil and Colombia, is virtually all concentrated in one or two regions (Ferreira and Gignoux 2011:

652). Many nation-states of Latin America are currently more spatially polarized economically than the EU-27, in GDP per capita terms. The current EU inter-national range is 4:1, between Ireland and Bulgaria, whereas provincial disparities amount to ratios of 9:1 in Brazil, 8:1 in Argentina, and 6:1 in Mexico (CEPAL 2010: 135). Between France and Algeria, the ratio is 3:1.

Four Mechanisms of (In)Equality

While most public discussion on inequality is concerned with results and patterns, policy wonks as well as social analysts are also interested in mechanisms. How are current inequalities produced? In what ways could equalization be produced?

The pioneer of this kind of perspective was the late great sociologist-*cum*-historian Charles Tilly (1998), with his study of enduring inequality in countries like South Africa and Northern Ireland. Tilly focused on a particularly vicious form of (economic) inequality, deriving from an asymmetrical pairing of racial/ethnic or ethno-religious categories, such as Whites and Blacks, or Protestants and Catholics. But for a more general understanding of how inequalities are generated, we need a wider view and a more general approach.

Ideologically, the analysis has often been strung up between '[individual] achievement' and 'exploitation' (cf. Wright 1994), or between inequality of outcome and equality of opportunity. I would argue that what is called 'achievement' is in fact very dependent on systemic game construction and reward structuration (as highlighted in table 2 above), while 'exploitation' is currently less important than Marx would have expected, and, thirdly, that 'equality of opportunity' is no more, and no less, than a time dimension of (in)equality. Again, the perspectives on offer are too narrow.

Inequalities are produced and sustained socially by systemic arrangements and processes, and by distributive action, individual as well as collective. It is crucial to pay systematic attention to both. 'Distributive action' is here taken as any social action, individual as well as collective, with direct distributive consequences, be they actions of systemic advance or retardation, or of allocation/redistribution. Together, distributive action and system dynamics produce and maintain inequalities through four different mechanisms, with different implications for evaluation and for change. The mechanisms refer to the kind of social process which yields a certain distributive outcome. They operate among kids at school as well as among regions of the world economy.

The processes are hung up between two poles of social interaction. At one pole we have the distance produced by A moving ahead of B, because of A's more helpful parents or other better preconditions, more training, lucky start/course, or harder effort. B is falling behind, because he did not see the new short-cut opened up, because he did not know that new means of production or transport had become available, or due to bad health, or for some other reason. No interaction between A and B is necessary to produce the distance between them, but both can see it and find it important. And, whatever produced the initial distance, it is not easy to catch up, and an uneven distribution of information and the social psychology of self-confidence, ambition and dedication often tend to consolidate and to widen it. We may refer to the process at that pole as *distanciation*. In liberal, individualist discourse, this mechanism is often referred to as 'achievement', and held to produce not inequality but legitimate rewards.

Distanciation is an important mechanism of inequality, which should not be subsumed under other processes. But 'achievement' would be a notion with ideological blinkers here. It is blind to everything but the achieving actor, telling us nothing about her relations to / dependence on others, about the social script defining 'achievement', or about the contexts of opportunities and rewards. While distanciation is one mechanism generating inequality, social distance may be a difference and not an inequality, in the sense we laid out above. Social distance is considered unjust, an inequality, by the disadvantaged and/or by observers to the extent that it indicates a distance between the actual lives of the disadvantaged and a possible, preferable one for them.

Distanciation is, first of all, a systemic process, in systems geared to producing winners and losers – including defining what constitutes 'winning' – and a distance of rewards and advantages between them. But systems, from schools to states and world economies, differ in their length of separation, their social distance between winners and losers, front-runners and laggards, the 'advanced' and the 'backward'. It is important to emphasize the systemic context of distanciation, as opposed to all the individualist ideology, that success is the singular achievement of the successful individual. But there are also other contextual variables besides systemic arrangements.

Human beings emerge as adult actors with different health and vigour produced by their childhood. Actors differ in their self-confidence facing risks and uncertainty, and they have differential access to information on new opportunities. In this way, through actor formation, social distances – of school achievement, job careers, social standing – tend to be reproduced over generations. In complex societies, there is always room for some individual 'working the system', but occasional cases of individual distancing from the crowd do not per se nullify an overall pattern of inequality. In periods of systemic change, such as the recent one from Communist socialism to capitalism, the process of distanciation strikes out in a new direction. The big winners, like the Russian 'oligarchs', seem to have been mainly marginal insiders, with elite education, socially connected but outside the political *Nomenklatura*, in Russia often for anti-Semitic reasons (cf. Chua 2003).

At the other pole of inequality mechanisms, A derives her advantages over B because of the valuables that B provides her with. At this pole we have inequality by *exploitation*. Exploitation involves a categorical division between some superior and some inferior people, whereby the former unilaterally or asymmetrically extract values from the latter. Freedom and property versus unfreedom and propertylessness has been the classical categorical divide underlying economic exploitation. Slavery and serfdom were classical examples. Marx argued that behind the labour–wage exchange a similar process of exploitation operated in capitalist markets, or rather in capitalist workplaces, providing capitalist property-owners with a surplus value, the basis of their profits.

That capitalist production is based on an asymmetrical appropriation of the fruits of human labour, and in this sense on exploitation, will be rather non-controversial among egalitarians. That the workers of Chinese, Bangladeshi or other tricontinental sweatshops producing for Walmart and other American or European retailers and brands are exploited few decent observers would deny. But the labour theory of value, at the root of Marxian economics, taken from Ricardo, is no longer held to be a tenable foundation for capitalist economics. This means that the prevalence and the amount of capitalist economic exploitation cannot be assessed empirically, nor can it be an axiom that all capital–wage labour relations are exploitative.[11]

---

[11] A radical American economist, John Roemer (1982), not so long ago made an attempt to rescue the Marxian concept

On the other hand, Marxism does not have a patent on 'exploitation'. It can be defined socially, as above, without any reference to economic theory, and it is widely used in social and social-psychological discourse. It bears clearly and heavily on existential inequality. We all know what exploiting another person's love, respect or admiration means: using it for our own advantage and giving nothing or little in return. While not always observable and seldom exactly calculable, exploitation is in principle empirically investigable. It remains a pillar of inequality analysis, albeit not as central as it was in the ancient tributary empires, or when it sustained American plantation slavery and Russian serfdom.

Exploitation is universally regarded as the worst form of inequality. Once some notion of elementary human equality has been accepted, exploitation is always unjust. In that sense, the very concept is normatively charged. It can be denied, or disguised as benevolent exchange, but it cannot be defended. Indeed, the concept's heavy load of moral opprobrium has restricted its practical economic employability. Few North Atlantic industrial workers today would think of themselves as exploited – other than on specific occasions – and the concept of exploitation has since long dropped out of the central rhetoric of the labour movement.

of exploitation, independently of the labour theory of value. While carried out with the author's characteristic mathematical aplomb, it ultimately depends on a thought experiment of economic withdrawal. If workers would be better off withdrawing from capitalism, taking their per capita share of the means of production with them, then they are exploited. This is pure economics at its best, brilliant, elegant, mathematically rigorous, and without much use in the messy empirical world. The author is still a fellow egalitarian, but to my knowledge he has lately been more preoccupied with inequality of opportunity than with exploitation.

Between distanciation and exploitation we can discern two other kinds of mechanisms producing inequalities. *Exclusion* means barring the advance or access of others, a divide of in-groups and out-groups. As an explanatory mechanism, exclusion had better be seen as a variable, rather than as a category, as a set of hurdles being placed in front of some people, a set which includes hindrances, 'glass ceilings', discriminations of various sorts, as well as closed gates. Exclusion figures in economics as monopolization, land rent and other kinds of 'rent-seeking' (cf. Sorensen 1996). French empirical sociology in the 1990s made it into a major, policy-pertinent social category in France (Paugam 1996) and in the EU, which, since its Laeken Council in 2001, has endorsed a set of indicators for measuring it. Stigmatization is a marker of exclusion, bestowing upon those outside never-healing cultural wounds.

We also have a kind of inequality deriving from some institutionalized ranking of social actors, some high, others low, from some super- and sub-ordination. It refers primarily to a ranking of the included, those inside the door of exclusion, but also the excluded may be ranked, as the inhabitants of Dante's *Inferno*. This is inequality by *hierarchization*, highlighting the importance of formal organization. Above, we took note of the potency of hierarchization, in its patterning of early death in the Whitehall government bureaucracy. An interesting modern example, no doubt inspired by ancestral tradition, was the system of civil service ranking set up in Communist China in 1953. It was a ladder with twenty-six ranks, which governed not only your salary, the appearance of your uniform, and the size and amenities of your apartment, but also your access to information and your means of travel on duty. Only from grade 14 and above could you buy a plane ticket or a comfortable, 'soft' train seat, and only from grade 13 could you book a hotel room with a private toilet (Chang 1991: 240–1). This hierarchical system was done away with in the 1960s (Zhou and Qin 2012: 48–9).

Hierarchization can also be anchored in an articulated value system. Pre-modern social orders were usually perceived and formulated in terms of hierarchical orders, estates or castes, with a core division of intellectuals (priests, Brahmins, Mandarins, ulama), warriors, traders/craftsmen and farmers. A similar hierarchy survived into contemporary high cultures through aesthetic value systems of 'taste' and 'style'. In contemporary Europe, this cultural hierarchization is probably most articulate in France, and Pierre Bourdieu (1979) devoted perhaps his very best work to it. He started from something which is no longer so self-evident, especially not outside France: 'To the socially recognized hierarchy of the arts . . . corresponds the social hierarchy of [their] consumers', whereby cultural tastes can function as 'privileged markers of "class"' (pp. I–II).

These four mechanisms are cumulative in their mode of operation. The exclusion mechanism becomes relevant and important to the extent that the excluding barriers or hindering obstacles are put up by those who are some sense ahead of and more advantaged than – at a distance from – others. For hierarchization to be institutionalized, some dividing barrier between superiors and inferiors must be in place. Exploitation, finally, presupposes distanciation, exclusion and institutionalized superiority/inferiority (though not necessarily a graded chain of command), and then adds on top of all that an extraction of resources from the inferiors. Exclusion, super-/sub-ordination and exploitation are all transitive mechanisms of inequality, mechanisms which, in contrast to distanciation, directly disadvantage the disadvantaged.

The mechanisms are not exclusive of each other. Any given distributive outcome may very well be the result of two or more mechanisms. Having worked with these mechanisms for about a decade, I tend to think that together these four can account for the generation of all kinds of inequality. But since they are tools of under-standing and analysis, I would not take it as failure if someone discovered more mechanisms.

The four mechanisms identified operate on health and life expectancy as well as on autonomy, recognition and respect, and on economic and other resources. Their relative weight may be assessed and debated with respect to any given distribution, from national income in the world economy to life expectancy in London or existential gender relations in an Indian village.

We may tabulate the mechanisms as in table 4, exem-plifying their dynamics, through systemic organization as well as through the direct-actor agency of individual or group actors.

Any comprehensive analysis of inequality should pay attention also to how inequality can be overcome, or at least reduced. To each of the mechanisms of inequality, there is in fact a corresponding kind of opposite mecha-nism: equality mechanisms.

To distanciation corresponds approximation, or catching-up, from the side of equality. Like their oppo-sites, equality mechanisms operate both through direct agency and through systemic arrangements. The most important of systemic approximations is affirmative action, sometimes also called 'positive discrimination'. It has been practised on a massive scale in India, reserv-ing educational places and public jobs for 'backward' castes and tribes (see further Galanter 1984). In the US since the breakthrough of the Civil Rights movement in the 1960s, it has been used to facilitate the entrance of Blacks into higher education, an arrangement very recently adopted in Brazil. Other systemic means of social approximation include providing poor parents with incentives for vaccination and other preventive

Table 4   *Inequality mechanisms and their interactive dynamics*

Mechanism	Dynamics	
	Direct agency	*Systemic dynamics*
Distanciation	Running ahead/ falling behind Outcompeting Social psychology of success/ failure	Reward structuration and normation, e.g. 'Winner takes all', 'Matthew effect', 'Star' system Returns to scale Information/ opportunity structuration
Exclusion	Closure, hindering, opportunity hoarding discrimination, monopolization	Membership boundaries, entry thresholds Cumulation of advantages Stigmatization Citizenship/property rights
Hierarchization	Super-/sub- ordination Patron/client relations Put down/ deference	Organizational ladder, status/ authority distance Hierarchy of family roles Systemic centre and peripheries Ethnic/racial/gendered hierarchies Generalizations of superiority/ inferiority
Exploitation	Extraction Utilization Abuse	Polarized power relations Asymmetric dependence Tributary systems

child care, and for sending their children to school. Extra teaching resources may be allocated to schools in disadvantaged areas.

The obvious opposite to exclusion is inclusion, opening the doors to membership, providing the previously excluded with rights, substituting rules against discrimination for barriers of exclusion. Hierarchies can be dismantled or flattened. They can be perforated by opening channels of internal qualification and advancement – e.g. of medical orderlies to nurses, of nurses to doctors – or they can be reduced and temporarily suspended by countervailing powers of the subordinates. That is what trade unions, collective bargaining and works councils like the German *Betriebsräte*, or student representatives on university bodies, mean. In formal organizations, from enterprises to churches, from universities to political parties, de-hierarchization has often been fought for under banners of 'democratization'. Capitalist market economies can be significantly de-hierarchized by rules facilitating and protecting the right to form trade unions, by labour rights enforceable by courts, and by minimum-wage legislation, putting a floor under how far down the wage-scale the most vulnerable workers can be pushed.

Exploitation can be counterposed to or overturned by redistribution, which, as we shall see below, has become a massive feature of contemporary advanced capitalism. In the existential field, the corresponding concept is more often rehabilitation, usually with apologies or self-criticism, which may be accompanied by economic compensation. In recent decades, rehabilitation has become a large-scale process.

Egalitarians have no shortage of means to reduce and overcome inequalities (table 5).

Catching-up may be due mainly to extra efforts, but on a larger scale it is usually dependent on context or system changes, which, of course, do not render efforts

Table 5   *Equality mechanisms*

	Direct agency	System dynamics
Approximation	Catching-up Using new opportunities	Compensatory capacitation Affirmative action
Inclusion	Migration Claiming membership	Entitlements, human rights Anti-discrimination laws
De-hierarchization	Collective organizing Collective bargaining Networking	Empowerment, democratization Organizational/ institutional flattening Internal re-qualification possibilities
Redistribution & *Rehabilitation*	Political organization & demands Philanthropy Political organization & demands	Taxation, social transfers & services Public rectification, compensation

without significance. Catching-up may also start from new systemic opportunities, for instance new technologies or new markets, to which latecomers may be faster to adapt. In economic history, such 'advantages of backwardness' were highlighted by the Harvard economic historian Alexander Gerschenkron (1962), drawing upon the nineteenth-century industrialization of Central and Eastern Europe East Asian economic development after World War II might be seen in a similar perspective.

Inclusion is perhaps the most widespread of the equality mechanisms. It is intrinsic to the modern nation-state, which entitles its citizens, and normally also its permanent residents, to certain rights and public services. To gain EU membership from 2004, the new member states had each to provide a National Action Plan on Social Inclusion. On a global scale, the discourse of and the public attention to human rights aim at an inclusion of humankind. A more tangible human inclusion has been the worldwide diffusion of medical knowledge and medical practice, with major effects on vital inequality in the world. Migrants migrate to get included in a context of better life-chances, in a resourceful city, or in a rich country. Claiming membership has been another extremely important direct action for inclusion – claiming the right to vote perhaps above all.

Trade union organizing and demanding collective bargaining on an equal level with the bosses has been a crucial challenge to modern organizational hierarchy. Organizational/institutional flattening has become a significant management doctrine in the latter area in recent decades, largely inspired by post-World War II Japanese management, and by the cultural upheaval following upon the student rebellions of the 1960s (cf. Boltanski and Chiapello 2007). Movements of organizational democratization were a central part of '1968', following upon a century of working-class struggles for trade union rights. Paradoxically, anti-hierarchical management ideology has since the 1980s run parallel to, and increasingly been overshadowed by, de-unionization drives. In academia, managerial hierarchies are increasingly supplanting democratic institutions.

The recent partial substitution, or at least supplementing, of hierarchy by horizontal networks is another mechanism of equality (cf. Castells 1998). However, it should not be forgotten that there are also vertical hierarchical networks of clientelism outside formal organizational structures.

Table 6 *The power of income redistribution*
Gini coefficients of market income and disposable income after taxes and transfers.

Country	Market income	Disposable income	Redistributive power: per cent reduction of inequality
Canada	41	32	22
Finland	39	24	38
Germany	40	28	31
Poland	47	33	29
Sweden	37	22	40
Great Britain	45	35	23
USA	45	37	18
Argentina (urban)	50	47	6
Bolivia	48	47	2
Brazil	57	54	5
Mexico	55	53	4
Peru	50	49	2

Note: OECD figures refer to 2004–5, Latin American (incl. Mexican) refer to 2008–9
Sources: OECD: OECD (2011a: table 7.3); Latin America: Lustig et al. (2012a: table 1)

Redistribution has been the main Social Democratic road to more equality, but it has had a wide political diffusion. It has been powerful and comparatively successful.

Social transfers, much more than taxes (which finance the former), are the main instrument of redistribution. They have been particularly important in reducing or, in the northwestern part of the European continent, largely doing away with, old-age poverty. But also with respect to income inequality among the working age (16–65) population, which de facto of course includes a substantial number of retirees, redistribution in the

OECD countries cuts income inequality by a quarter on average (OECD 2011a: figure 6.1).

Rehabilitation has become a significant feature of contemporary history. As a macro phenomenon, it began in the post-Stalinist Soviet Union and Eastern Europe, rehabilitating victims of political repression. While that had great political and moral significance, it is not quite within the field of (in)equality. More pertinent to the latter have been rehabilitations of the victims of modernist developmentalism and a recognition of the existential equality of indigenous peoples, of children of Aboriginal or just poor families taken away from their parents and farmed out to more 'civilized' or 'respectable' foster parents. Recent governments, from Australia to Sweden, have apologized to the victims, and compensation has been paid.

The relative importance of these mechanisms of inequality and equality is at the centre of scholarly as well as political controversies about world development, although the mechanisms are usually only implied in area-specific notions, reflecting the under-theorized field of inequality. Did world inequality arise mainly because of distanciation at the time of the Industrial Revolution, with the North Atlantic economies running ahead and away? Or was it also due to hindering exclusive practices, like the crowding-out of Indian manufactures by the British rulers, the violent 'opening' of China, the hierarchization of the whole world into a 'civilized' colonizing part and an 'uncivilized' colonized part? To what extent was Western European prosperity, and its initial industrial advantage, built upon colonial exploitation, of the Americas in particular? Is the recent widening of income differentials in the US and elsewhere due to technological change and to ensuing labour demand shifts, widening the distance between the high- and the low-skilled, or is it significantly an effect of the excluding processes of a social and political disorganization of the popular classes?

III

History

Always more interested in the present and its future, I opted for social science rather than history. But I have never stopped being fascinated by the location of the present in time, as well as in space. The late American Marxist scholar Paul Sweezy (1955) expressed it emblematically in a book title, *The Present as History*. Like the vast expanses of planetary space, the long arc of time teaches us an important sense of proportions, of limitations – a sense of political as well as scholarly humility – in facing the universe. But historical, as well as other-spatial, experiences can also provide sources of inspiration and courage. More prosaically, a historical perspective helps you to understand where you are, and what you can do.

5

Inequality and the Rise of Modernity

In pre-modern times there were differences, vertical differences – of free men and slaves, of kings, noblemen and commoners, of rich and poor – like there were differences of men and women and of young and old. Differences were not always accepted. The legitimacy of kings was quite often contested. Occasionally there were peasant uprisings, artisanal urban insurrections, even slave rebellions. Some revolts raised egalitarian demands, usually religiously motivated. But there was hardly any inequality, i.e., perceived, discussed, theorized in-equality. There was no this-worldly human commonality; there were no norms of some kind of this-worldly human equality.

With modernity, inequality became an issue, for two confluent reasons. One was the idea of historically changing and politically changeable society, which developed during the Enlightenment as a companion to the emergence of large-scale commercial capitalism. Before the eyes of Scottish historians, social philosophers and economists – from John Millar to Adam Smith – and of the contemporary French Physiocrats, agrarian societies – in particular, manorial ones – were overtaken or transformed by 'commerce', as hunting and gathering had once been by the advent of agriculture.

The other was a secular notion of some fundamental human equality. Christianity and Islam both had a theological conception of an equality of human souls, which radical heretics could sometimes invoke – before they were crushed. But now, in the course of the Enlightenment, visions of some this-worldly human equality emerged, in critiques of aristocratic privileges and of personal dependence and heteronomy as 'slavery' – though rarely concretely directed against actual slavery (cf. Rosanvallon 2011: part I; Blackburn 2011: chs 2–3). They were soon to provide the intellectual ammunition of the late eighteenth-century Atlantic revolutions.

Hereby in-equality became a political and a moral problem. Humans were no longer just different, of different rank, of different wealth, of different luck. Their equality could be violated; they could be un-equal. And if the societal constitution was changing, in what direction was it going? What was happening to (in)equality?

Three Master Narratives

In the history of modern social science, we may distinguish three major – in retrospect, 'classical' – very different answers to that question. Two were offered in the second third of the nineteenth century, while the third got its most influential formulation in the mid twentieth century. The main proponents of all three are still venerated, but, at least on the issue of inequality, none would today be accepted as a dispute-settling authority. They never met; nor have, as far as I know, their admirers.

The three classical master narratives of modern inequality have been, first, that it is continuously declining. Modernity is the era of evolving equality. Second, modernity means a polarization between the affluence of the few and the increasing misery of the many. The third story is that, in modern times, inequality first rises and then declines.

We owe the first interpretation to a remarkable French liberal aristocrat who, in the mid-1830s, went to visit the United States, and wrote a long love letter about it, which is often regarded as the first modern classic of political science: *De la démocratie en Amérique* (*On Democracy in America*). With his background experience, de Tocqueville (1840/1961, II: 452) was overwhelmed by American egalitarianism, which he extrapolated into a world history of modernity: 'I see that goods and bads are allocated rather equally in the world. Great wealths are disappearing, the number of small fortunes is growing; desires and pleasures are multiplying; there are no longer extraordinary prosperities nor miseries without remedy.' Tocqueville's second major book, *The Ancien Régime & the French Revolution* (1856) was, naturally, less starry-eyed, but his feed into the liberal American *mythos* remains a very important interpretation of modern history.

Writing only a couple of decades later, the exiled German Communist Karl Marx drew an absolutely opposite conclusion. This was the epoch of capitalist economics, and capitalism meant inherent tendencies of mounting inequality: 'With the ever declining number of capital magnates, who usurp and monopolize all the advantages of this transformation process, the mass of misery, pressure, subjugation, degeneration and exploitation is growing. . . .' (*Das Kapital* – Marx 1867/1921, I: 728).

It is a sobering thought for social diagnostics, that two such brilliant scholars could perceive the world so differently. They looked at the world from very different perspectives of time, and had different objects, as well as objectives, on their mind: de Tocqueville focused on the outcomes of the two great eighteenth-century revolutions, the French and the American. He was mainly interested in politics and in law. Politically, he was a Liberal, at ease in the Liberal July Monarchy. Marx concentrated on analysing the new economic system coming out of the Industrial Revolution, in the wake of the dismantling of the aristocratic order. His search light centred on the socioeconomic conditions of a new class, the industrial proletariat. As a Socialist intellectual his political objective was to rouse the new working class into action. The two analysts were looking primarily at different countries: de Tocqueville at France and the USA, Marx at Britain.

To a large extent, then, de Tocqueville and Marx were talking past each other, and later historiography of social science has hardly ever tried to relate and compare them. However, from their radically different starting-points, the diagnoses of de Tocqueville and Marx did meet on the same ground, as the quotations above illustrate. So, who was right, and who was wrong?

They both were, we may say, with the hindsight of latter-day research: de Tocqueville was right in highlighting that the French Revolution had done away with the legal and political inequalities of caste and estate of the *ancien régime*, and that the rising power of the United States was in the first half of the nineteenth century in most respects – except for Southern slavery and for the Western genocide of the Indians – much more equal than the Old World of Europe. Moreover, the French Revolution had cut down economic inequality, a result not fully undone by the Restoration or by the July Monarchy (Morrisson 2000: table 7b).

Nineteenth-century Britain was one of the most unequal countries of the North Atlantic, clearly more so than Prussia, but on a par with post-revolutionary France (Lindert 2000: table 1, and Morrisson 2000: tables 6c and 7b). It was home to the 'dark satanic mills' (William Blake) of early industrialism. There was a significant long-term rise in the real income share of the richest 5 per cent in England and Wales in the period from the mid eighteenth century until the eve of World War I, and a marked increase in the wealth share of the top 1 per cent from the early eighteenth century until about 1875, after which it stayed on a high plateau until the mid-1920s (Lindert 2000: 179ff.).

Capitalist industrialization generally produced more inequality in Europe, as in France of the 1830s–1860s and Germany after 1870 (Morrisson 2000: 234, 236). In Sweden and the Netherlands, economic inequality began to rise early – in Sweden, as in England, already in the eighteenth century, and in the Netherlands in the seventeenth (Morrisson 2000: 229, 238). In the United States, inequality augmented strongly in the course of the nineteenth century, although the turning-points of the distribution curve have not yet been exactly dated, although recent expert evaluation is that US inequality turned for the worse at the time of de Tocqueville's visit (Floud et al. 2011: 330; Fogel 2012: 30). US inequality of health and life expectancy also increased between 1790 and 1870 (Lindert 2000: 192).

In sum, Marx was also right, and, with regard to socioeconomic conditions, more so than de Tocqueville, but he overplayed the drama, and did not foresee the relative social stabilization of industrial capitalism around 1900. It would not be illuminating to end by putting Karl Marx on a pedestal of winning correctness. We also know by now that the Marxian tendency of polarization did not continue in the twentieth century. It did go on inter-nationally (globally until the 1950s – between the richest and the poorest countries it is still ongoing), but nationally, within all the centres of capitalism, it was reversed, into equalization. This reversal started in Europe with World War I and in the USA with the Depression of the 1930s, and reigned until the oil crisis of the 1970s, although its concrete trajectories varied across nations.

Tocqueville blew up post-feudal existential equalization into an ancient trend of historical evolution as well as a modern 'passion' (1840/1961, II: Second Part). But he did spot an important historical change, which Marx in his communitarian war against liberal individualism never quite recognized, in spite of the *Communist Manifesto*'s tribute to the modern revolution of the bourgeoisie. Marx was more concerned with human emancipation and capability of development than with equality of conditions.

While de Tocqueville saw the modern world, with a mixture of respect, resignation and worry, as one of fatally mounting equality, and Marx, anticipating a future revolution, saw it as a society of accelerating inequality, our third master, Simon Kuznets (1955), saw industrial modernity as first increasing inequality, and then decreasing it. Kuznets was a Russian-American economist, and later a Nobel Laureate. His most famous paper was his Presidential Address to the American Economic Association. At the time of his writing, this was, on the whole, an adequate picture of the economic history of North Atlantic capitalism. In contrast to the nineteenth-century prophets, Kuznets was a cautious academic who formulated his picture as a 'conjecture'. Allowing for nationally variable time scales, Kuznets believed that, in modern time, inequality took the shape of an inverted U-curve (figure 1). Economic growth and industrialization first meant that the share of people in high productivity sectors, with high income, increased, leading to higher overall inequality. Later, with further economic growth, the rest of the population would

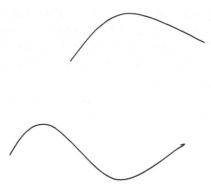

Figure 1   *Stylized income inequality curves of developed countries, mid-nineteenth to late twentieth centuries*
Top: the stylized Kuznets Curve of Modernization, inequality first rising, then declining.
Bottom: the stylized actual curve of late nineteenth- to twentieth-century inequality in the rich countries, best illustrated by the UK and the US.
Sources: Kuznets (1955); Cornia (2004); Atkinson and Piketty (2010)

catch up, and inequality would fall. To his great credit, Kuznets himself did not present this as a master narrative of 'modernization'. On the contrary, he warned against the possibility that industrialization in the underdeveloped countries might be an even more traumatic, socially and politically dislocating and inegalitarian affair than in earlier ones, like Britain, because of their seemingly more unequal starting-point.

How well Kuznets captured the actual distributive processes of the short twentieth century has been debated among economists as well as among historians, and need not concern us here, although the widespread acceptance of his hypothesis should be noticed. Less remembered and heeded is the end of his address, calling for 'a shift from market economics to political and social economy'. What is undeniable, though, is that, from about 1980, the overwhelming, if not universal, tendency of the centres of capitalism has been one of rising income inequality. The curve is bending upwards again (Cornia 2004).

In other words, the legacy of the outgoing twentieth century was a return of inequality.

6

A Historical Six-Pack: Three Inequalities in Global and National History

After looking up into the theoretical stratosphere of grand social theory, we shall make a little excursion with a historical six-pack. Above, we have distinguished three kinds of inequality, vital, existential and resource. How can we summarize their modern development, globally and nationally?

Vital Inequality

The daring long-distance historian Angus Maddison (2001: 29ff.) has argued that, already by the mid sixteenth century, English life expectancy was well ahead of the world, England being joined in the eighteenth century by Sweden, Japan and USA, and by France after the Revolution. The gap between this group (and other Western European countries) and the rest of the world then widened until around 1950. That view is supported by comparative evidence from India and the UK (Therborn 2006: table 1.4). Infant mortality, for which there are more data, gives the same picture, for instance between, on the one hand, the USA – both Black and White – and, on the other, Argentina and other South American countries, although Mexico after its revolution diminished the mortality gap between it and the US (Mitchell 1998: table A7). Distanciation was driven by advances in the rich nations. At least from the mid twentieth century, a process of equalization started, coeval with Asian decolonization and the beginning of global health and development concerns and support for vaccination, malaria eradication, etc.

Around 1990 this process stopped, for two reasons. One was the AIDS epidemic in sub-Saharan Africa; the other was the restoration of capitalism in the former Soviet Union (Stuckler et al. 2009; Cornia and Menchini 2006). Both reduced life expectancy dramatically, while the rest of world continued to improve. In the worst-hit southern African countries, life expectancy at birth was, in 2000–5, fifteen years shorter in Zimbabwe than in 1970 to 1975–6, eleven years shorter in Zambia. The Russian overall decline was four years for both sexes, but much higher for males. (UNDP 2007: table 10). Between the implosion of the Soviet Union in 1991 and 1994, male life expectancy in Russia went down by seven years (Shkolnikov et al. 2001: figure 1).

Since about 2000, both the ex-USSR and Africa are recovering, but, by 2009, mortality in Zambia and Zimbabwe is still higher than it was in the 1970s, and in South Africa life expectancy is eight years below its 1990 level. In Russia, it is still a year shorter than in 1990 – in the Ukraine, two years, and three for males (WHO 2012: table 1). In terms of life expectancy at birth, there is on the whole a weak tendency of global convergence going on, though with Africa so far excepted. With respect to child mortality, absolute differences are decreasing, between Africa and the rest included, but ratios of survival are widening.

Within nations, on the other hand, available evidence points strongly to a different trajectory of vital inequality – that is, to a stability of class inequality of life and health over the past 100 years, with a rising tendency in recent times. Even the Scandinavian welfare states have failed to assure vital equality among classes (Kunst 1997; Vågerö 2006). A rare nineteenth-century datum, from Copenhagen in 1865–74 (Westergaard 1901), indicates a class differential of age-standardized mortality, of around 2:1 between manual workers and upper-white-collar strata, which looks quite similar to British class data for 1991–3: 2.9 for unskilled and 1.8 for semi-skilled manual to professional (Westergaard 1901; Fitzpatrick and Chandola 2000: table 3.8).[12]

There is also the strange history of American bodies, pointing to mounting inequality in the nineteenth century. Native-born American free males shrank in average height from the 1830s to 1890, and seem only to have recovered their 1780 height by 1920 (army veterans data; Floud et al. 2011: table 6.10). The two main explanations on offer for this extraordinary trajectory are: first, urbanization, because cities in the nineteenth century, in contrast to in the poor world today, were more dangerous to your health (if you were poor) than the countryside; and, second, immigrant heritage of parental poverty (Fogel 2012: 30).

Britain has the best class-differentiated vital statistics. There, the class inequality of dying between ages 20 and 44 clearly increased between 1910–12 and 1991–3 (Fitzpatrick and Chandola 2000: table 3.8). And it keeps growing (Marmot 2012). In London, the gap in

---

[12] The data are not exactly comparable. Apart from possible differences of occupational classification, Danish mortality refers to men 25–75, the English to men 20–44. I am grateful to my Finnish demographer colleague Pekka Martikainen for supplying me with the Copenhagen data.

History

male life expectancy between upper-middle-class Chelsea and Kensington and poor Tottenham Green is now seventeen years (*Guardian*, 11 February 2012, p. 6), which is the same size as that between the UK and Myanmar (WHO 2012: table 1). Between the thirty-three boroughs of London, the range of male life expectancy has widened from 5.4 years in 1999–2001 to 9.2 years in 2006–8 (London Health Observatory 2011). If you travel east on the underground Jubilee line, life expectancy of the residents is decreasing by half a year at every stop (London Health Observatory 2011).

The reasons for this enduring, even increasing, class inequality of life and health, which is more pronounced among men than among women but which has the same pattern among the latter, are most likely several. At the bottom are psychosomatic consequences of different class or status situations. Lack of respect and lack of control of your life and work situation are bad for your health and increase your risk of premature death. This has been demonstrated in a large longitudinal study of employees at Whitehall, the central government offices in Britain, from janitors to top civil servants. The odds of premature death and of ill-health were found to follow closely the bureaucratic ladder: the higher your position, the lower your risk of dying. This correlation turned out to be little affected by 'lifestyle' controls, for use of tobacco and alcohol (Marmot 2004: ch. 2).

For recent increases in vital inequality, there are two main suspects. One is increasing economic uncertainty and polarization, between the unemployed and the labour market marginalized, on the one hand, and the surfers on the boom waves, on the other. The other is nowadays often called 'lifestyle', but is better termed 'life-options'. It is not so much a choice of style as a perspective of possible options. People who have little control of their basic life situation, of finding a job, of controlling their work context, of launching a life-course career, may be expected to be less prone to control the health of their bodies – to notice and to follow expert advice on tobacco, alcohol and other drugs, on diet and exercise – than people who have a sense of controlling their own lives.

Existential Inequality

Here again there has been a non-linear historical development (figure 2). Racism grew with nineteenth-century imperialism, far away from the global oecumenism of Voltaire and Herder. It reached its climax with the Nazi German Holocaust. After 1945, existential inequality has been in steep decline internationally. The 1948 UN Declaration of Human Rights set a global agenda of fundamental existential equality, which has evolved gradually. Racism was discredited by its World War II defeat and by the horror of Auschwitz. Sexism came under global attack in the 1970s, with the UN Women's Conference in Mexico and its ensuing Women and Development Decade. Pre-modern indigenous populations, sometimes called First Nations, appeared on the

Baseline 1900
Universal, if differentiated, patriarchy, worldwide
   Euro-American colonialism, universally reigning
   institutionalized racism of White supremacy, predominant
   worldwide conception of hierarchy of human existence.

1910s
Dismantling of legal patriarchy in Scandinavia and in
   revolutionary Russia.
After World War I, North Atlantic establishment of civic
   equality – male only in the Latin regions.

Figure 2 *Landmarks of existential (in)equality, 1900–2012*

1920s
Rise and defeats of anti-racist movements in Asia and
   Africa; rise of pro-indigenous cultural movement in
   Latin America, above all in Mexico.
Tightened racist immigration legislation in USA.
Women first denied then recognized as 'persons' in imperial
   law of Canada.

1930s – World War II
Nazi German official racism and genocide.
During World War II, domestic genocidal operations, from
   the Baltics to Croatia and Romania.
Widespread diffusion and policy application of eugenics,
   including in Scandinavia.

1945–1950
Discrediting of explicit racism, but victory in South Africa.
Asian decolonization.
UN Declaration of Human Rights.
Dismantling of legal patriarchy in East Asia and Eastern
   Europe.
Civic rights of women in Latin Europe, and, gradually, in
   Latin America.

1950s
Caste discrimination legally proscribed in India, beginning
   of affirmative action for 'Scheduled Castes'.
Racist school segregation declared unconstitutional in USA.
Western European gradual dismantling of Poor Law-type
   quasi-penal treatment of the elderly, the infirm, orphans.

1960s
African decolonization.
Global anti-authoritarian student movement.
US Civil Rights movement, American universal right to vote
   and right to inter-racial marriage.
UN Convention against Racial Discrimination.
Erosion of racist immigration legislation in North America
   and Oceania.

Figure 2   *Continued*

1970s–1980s
Tide of global Feminism, UN Decade for Women,
  inter-continental dismantling or delimiting of
  institutionalized patriarchy.
Legal gender equality in all Western Europe.
De-racialization of immigration to USA, Canada, Australia,
  New Zealand.
Universal suffrage in Brazil.

1990s
End of apartheid in South Africa.
Violent ethnic conflicts in the wake of the break-up of
  the multinational Communist states of the USSR and
  Yugoslavia.
Genocide in Rwanda.
Widespread struggles for respect for existential difference
  and equality, of ethnicity, gender and sexuality.
UN Conference of Women in Beijing in 1995.
Beginning recognition of sexual equality, with
  breakthroughs in Western Europe and South Africa.
Delimited patriarchal backlash – Muslim, Jewish,
  Christian.
Mounting anti-immigration racism in Europe.

2000s–early 2010s
Rise of indigenous movements, above all in Indo-America
  and in India.
UN Declaration on the Rights of Indigenous Peoples.
'Plurinational' constitution in Bolivia.
Movements and recognitions of 'Afro-descendentes' rising
  in Brazil and other parts of South America.
Successful low-caste politics in India.
Same-sex marriage being recognized in parts of the
  Americas and of Western Europe, and in Nepal.
Continuous advances of women, in higher education,
  corporate leadership, politics, military.

Figure 2 *Continued*

global stage in the 1990s, acquiring some respect for their non-modern ways of life. The last third of the past century was a period of major existential equalization globally.

The global mainstream has clearly moved into existential equalization after 1945, and equalization of personal autonomy, recognition and respect remains the main tendency of today's world. This development tends to get lost in the preoccupations with the income of the 1 per cent. However, it has not been a gradual human evolution of modernity. The worst genocides in history took place rather recently, in the 1940s and in the 1990s. There has been significant backlash against women's rights and against immigrants. Anti-Semitism is still alive (*European Societies* 2012), Islamophobia has spread in Europe and North America, and anti-Arabism seems to be mounting among Israelis in Palestine. Patriarchy and misogyny are still ruling most of Africa and West and South Asia, often violently. There is resurgent hinterland patriarchy in China, and persistent male discrimination against women, e.g. on the labour market, still characterizes 'developed' East Asia.

Intra-national developments then vary, and they have not always followed the international calendar. From the late 1940s, South Africa turned into an explicit, pervasive racist regime, continuously growing worse until the 1970s. White racism survived 1945 in the Anglo-Saxon settler states of the USA and Australia. The US South remained racist one-party states until the late 1960s, and the Australian Labour Party kept its prime programmatic slogan – Keep Australia White – until the early 1970s. Indians of the Andean states of South America managed to step out of White and Mestizo shadows only in the 2000s.

Women's rights have made great strides in Europe and the Americas since the 1970s, largely driven by the movements of '1968'. But patriarchy and misogyny still remain predominant in most of Asia and of sub-Saharan Africa (Inglehart and Norris 2003; Therborn 2004: chs. 2–3). Contrary to common Western assumptions, it is not the Arab countries which are most sexist, but sub-Saharan Africa, India and the rest of South Asia (UNDP 2011: table 4).

Caste had evolved into a particularly pernicious denial of existential equality. Its dimension of occupational heritage was a general feature of pre-modern European and other societies, and so was its general status ranking. But Indian caste was also embedded in religious Hindu notions of pollution. Therefore, the lowest of the pyramid were the 'Untouchables', the unclean, whose very shadow could pollute a high-caste Hindu. Indian nationalism, with Gandhi at the forefront, campaigned against caste discrimination, which was banned after Independence. But, like so many laws of the weak state of India, it had little social impact. Marriage is still largely arranged according to caste, and low caste still means low class (for a recent overview, see Weisskopf 2011). However, the democracy of Indian politics has meant that the ex-Untouchables – now the *Dalits* – are sitting on a significant votebank. In 2006, in the most populous of the Indian states, a *Dalit*-led coalition, successfully courting also high-caste Brahmins, won the state election and provided the Chief Minister (Rao 2009: 281ff.).

Successful industrialization and the labour movement brought social respect to the working class in the rich countries. Successful development has also brought to the surface previously suppressed or ignored discriminations and humiliations, in the name of 'development'. Multiculturalism has come to involve recognition and respect of indigenous populations, 'First Nations' and their specific modes of life. The existential traumata of children captured by development agencies, 'in the best interests of the child', have recently been brought to

light by their now late-middle-aged or older victims –
for example poor children from Britain deported to the
White Dominions, Aboriginal children of Australia
taken from their parents into White 'civilization',
Swedish children of parents who were poor and/or held
to be dysfunctional farmed out to foster parents. There
are likely to be similar cases in many other countries.
Governments have belatedly apologized and paid out
compensation.

However, even though blatant, institutionalized existential inequality, such as racism, sexism and ruthless
developmentalism or 'civilizing' zeal, have been eroded,
existential inequality is still permeating contemporary
societies. Its enormous importance to health, sickness
and longevity has been demonstrated decisively, as we
noticed in the previous section. The research frontier at
the interface of sociology and medicine is busy making
new discoveries about it. A very recent example comes
from a longitudinal study of children born in Aberdeen,
Scotland, in the first half of the 1950s. It was found that
children who attended school classes with more unequal
sociometric status structures had more health problems
as mid-life adults than those who went to more sym-
metrical school classes. This difference held for the
cohorts as a whole, not only for the isolates at school
(Almquist 2011: paper 1), a strong vindication of
Richard Wilkinson's (Wilkinson 2005; Wilkinson and
Pickett, 2009) argument that inequality hurts also the
privileged.

There are also current social tendencies driving new
forms of existential inequality: de-industrialization outsourcing, immigration of the poor, and labour market
marginalizations. Such tendencies are now directed
against an 'underclass' of people marginalized or
excluded from the labour market, the second generation
of industrial immigrants, poor single mothers, the children of de-industrialized workers. In Britain, they have

been given a new pejorative identity as the 'chavs' (Jones 2011). In a US conservative bestseller portrait, they are a new 'lower class', unmarried, lazy, dishonest and godless (Murray 2012).

Class is here returning as an existential put-down.

Resource Inequality

Even more than the others, this dimension of inequality – in which we shall, above all, look at income – underlines the importance of distinguishing global and national trends.

Globally, there was a strong tendency towards increasing inequality, running from at least the early nineteenth up to the mid twentieth century, the 1950s–1960s. In that period, the modern conception of the 'civilized' vs the 'non-civilized' – after 1945, 'developed' as opposed to 'underdeveloped' – world was established. Asia was the main loser. Excluding Japan, the Asian share of world GDP declined from 56 per cent in 1820 to 15 per cent in 1950. At the other end, the Western European share went from a quarter in 1820 to a third in 1870 and 1913, back to a quarter by 1950. The USA produced at most 2 per cent of world production in 1820, but a fifth in 1913 and a good quarter in 1950. While Europe, east and west, was growing, together with the USA and Japan, and after 1870 Latin America – and for 1913–50, Africa as well – China and India were stagnating or declining in the nineteenth century, and both clearly declining for 1913–50 (Maddison 2001: tables B-20 and B-22).

Income

The World Bank economist Branko Milanovic has distinguished three global measures of income inequality.

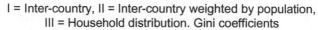

I = Inter-country, II = Inter-country weighted by population,
III = Household distribution. Gini coefficients

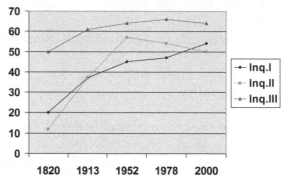

Figure 3   *Global income inequality, 1820–2000*
Source: based on Milanovic (2005: ch. 11)

One is GDP per country capita. The second is GDP per
capita weighted by the population of the country,
making the poverty of a big poor country or the wealth
of a big rich country count more than that of a small
one. Both concepts have the disadvantage of assuming
that there is equality within countries. The third measure
tries to grasp within-country inequality as well, by using
household surveys instead of aggregate national
accounts. Piecing together the surveys and making them
comparable is a delicate and difficult task, which, in
spite of the heroic efforts of Milanovic and others,
cannot yet be regarded as quite solved. And historical
estimates of domestic distributions, before the collection
of any representative household surveys, is of course
extra hazardous. Nevertheless, the main historical tendencies are probably captured in figure 3.

In the mid twentieth century, the curve of inequality
flattened out, with the decolonization of India and the
independence of China, and recently with a down-
bending tendency, owing to the economic surge of huge

poor countries like China and India, and also to the vigorous post-2000 growth of the African poorhouse. But world polarization between countries has not stopped, in spite of current growth among the world's poorest states. In 2005 what the UN calls 'the least developed countries' had a per capita national income of about 16 per cent of world income. By 2011 that share had declined to 14 per cent (UNDP 2007: 246; UNDP 2011: table 10).

National trajectories took other paths. The nineteenth-century rise of industrial capitalism did, as Marx predicted and as we noticed above, generate more economic inequality, but not on a dramatic scale (cf. Lindert 2000). The twentieth century brought about major equalization, in Europe from World War I, in the USA from the Depression of 1929 and after. Outside the North Atlantic, other distributive winds were blowing in the twentieth century. East Asia, from US-occupied Japan to Communist China, embarked on equalization in the late 1940s, as did decolonized India. In Latin America, drastic equalizations took place in Peronist Argentina, but no secular trend seems to have been established.

Total inequality is usually driven from the top, by the share of the richest, rather than from below, by that of the poorest. Therefore, the great efforts by Tomas Piketty, Anthony Atkinson, Emmanuel Saez and their associates to create a global and historical overview of the share of top incomes constitute our best picture of intra-national income inequality in the world. Their data are basically official statistics of tax returns, and refer to pre-tax income, which in recent decades would not mean the same in countries of significant redistribution – including the USA – as in others, in Latin America and Asia, with little of it. But they do convey a unique world picture of inequality and its development over time.

Table 7 *Top incomes in the world, 1913–2005*

Per cent of total income appropriated by the top 1%, and/or the top 0.1% of income earners. The first figure for each entry refers to the income share of the top %, the second to the top 0.1%.

	1913	1929	1939	1949	2005
France	20, 8 (1919)	16, 6	13, 5	9, 3	8, 2
Germany	17, 8	11, 4	16, 7 (1938)	12, 4	11, 4
Spain	–	–, 1.4[a]	–, 1.3[b]	–, 0.8[c]	9, 3, 0.9[c]
Sweden	21, 9 (1912)	14, 5 (1930)	10, 3 (1941)	8, 2	6, 2
UK	19, 9 (1918)	–, 8	17, 7 (1937)	11, 3	14, 5
USA	18, 9	18, 8	15, 5	11, 3	18, 8
Argentina	–	–	21, 8	19, 8[d]	17, 7
Japan	17, 7	18, 8	18, 8	8, 2	9, 2
China	–	–	–	3 (1986), 0.5	6, 1
India	–	13, 6	16, 7	12, 5	9, 4 (1999)
Indonesia	–	17, 6	20, 7	–	–, 1[e]

[a] top 0.01% in 1933;
[b] top 0.01% in 1940;
[c] top 0.01%;
[d] in 1953, the corresponding figures were 15 and 5;
[e] top 0.01% in 2003.

Source: Atkinson and Piketty (2010: ch. 13)

On the eve of World War I, high inequality was universal, with Sweden the most unequal, where the richest 1 per cent took 21 per cent of all personal income, and the richest 0.1 per cent took 9 per cent. There was little difference between the USA and Europe. World War I and its aftermath constituted the first period of equalization in modern history (after the French Revolution). Naturally, it had its main effect in Europe, the continent ravaged by the war, but also in Sweden which managed to stay out of it.

The Depression of the 1930s had a very differentiated distributive impact: strong where the stock exchange crash issued into redistributive politics, as in the US with the New Deal, Sweden with Social Democracy, and France with the Popular Front. In Nazi Germany, the rich recovered, and they did not suffer in Spain with Franco's victory. The big Asian colonies of India and Indonesia became more unequal in the 1930s, whereas militarized Japan stayed put. The outcome of World War II was a major equalizer, not only in defeated Germany (figures here refer to West Germany) and Japan, but also among the victors, France, the UK and the US. Along a twisted national path, the war outcome was also behind the rise of Perón out of the originally pro-Fascist military junta, and his subsequent policies of equalization.

The British and the American figures for 2005 indicate a postwar bend in the curve of (in)equality, with a strong new increase in inequality between 1949 and 2005, actually turning upwards after 1980. In the USA, the richest 0.1 per cent then had an income share about the same as the top 1 per cent in France: almost 8 per cent. In the Netherlands, the one-thousandth at the top appropriated 1.1 per cent of national income, about the same as in its former colony Indonesia. Across most of the rich OECD world, although not in democratizing Spain, the deflection of the post-World War II curve of income inequality occurred around 1980, as the low point of inequality.

De-industrialization was clearly one major reason. It started in the second half of the 1960s and accelerated in the wake of the 1970s oil crisis, with its subsequent weakening of labour and of trade unions, which reached their maximum organization in the 1970s. The surge of financial capitalism, after the abandonment of the postwar Bretton Woods currency order, pushed ahead by the 1980s onslaught of financial deregulation, is another. The globalization of capitalism, with its inclusion of China, Vietnam and Eastern Europe, may be a third. We shall return to this causal tangle below (in chapter 8).

While powerful transnational forces were clearly at work, their impact has been divided between nations. Within the rich OECD we may distinguish between *U-countries* and *turned-around J-countries*, named after their twentieth-century curves of income distribution.

The U-countries are regressing to their pre-World War II inequality, whereas the J-countries more or less keep the historical gains of the popular classes after the World War, while stopping any further equalization, with most of them currently growing more unequal. The J group consists of continental Western Europe, Argentina and the Asian countries India, Indonesia, Japan.

The core of the U-countries are the members of the White former British empire – in this respect, as in all others, nowadays headed by the USA, followed by the UK. New Zealand, and probably by now – but by 2005, not quite – Australia and Canada, are also back to their pre-World War II levels of inequality.

What leads to this line-up is still largely unexplored, and not quite obvious, given the rather different economic and political structures of the countries, and also the different timing. While the US and the UK heartily embarked on inequalization in the 1980s, Canada was actually going in the opposite direction, in terms of disposable income, catching up with inequalization only from the mid-1990s, due to a right-wing policy turn on taxes and transfers (OECD 2011a: table A1.1).

Taken together with the turned-around J-countries of continental Western Europe and Japan, the pattern means that any overall notion of 'globalization' is a weak contender for general explanation. Income inequality – of disposable income after taxes and transfers – increased in virtually all rich countries from the mid-1980s to the mid-2000s, although with varying decadal emphasis. Sweden had an exceptionally strong surge in inequality from the mid-1990s, but from a low base, still keeping the country below the OECD average of inequality, but more unequal than Norway, Austria or ex-Czecho-Slovakia, and in the range of Germany and France (see table 10 below). Among the big European countries, Germany has had a substantial increase of inequality, while staying below the OECD average. France has been most successful at resisting the surge of inequality, actually decreasing it in the decade from the mid-1980s to the mid-1990s, leaving the country with a current inequality about equal to that of Germany.

Education

With respect to education, another resource, there has been a global process of equalization since 1980 (Goesling and Baker 2008: table 5). However, educational inequality is still huge in India (and the whole of South Asia) and in the Arab states (see table 8 below). Within-country inequality of education has also tended to decline (Thomas et al. 2000)

What the above surveys do not convey, however, are two important aspects of the divides of education, of growing importance because of the augmented value of formal education. One is the divide between private and public institutions of education. At the primary and the secondary levels, private schools are better – because they are much better equipped and selective – than public ones in most parts of the world, though not the tax-financed private schools in Sweden. The classical nation-state citizens' school is increasingly abandoned, even in Northern Europe. From very early on, children are segregated into different schools. At the university level, in some countries, the segregation operates in the opposite way, in Brazil in particular, but also partly in Chile, Japan and some states of the USA. The selective public universities offer the best education, and the children of less-educated parents, and/or of lower-income parents who cannot afford the private secondary schools, have to make do with shoddy, expensive profiteering outlets. In Chile, this system was introduced by the military dictatorship.

Second, what is coming increasingly into sight are the aggravating consequences of remaining educational divides, as we noticed in chapter 1. In the 21st-century 'knowledge economies', the low-educated are at an increasing disadvantage, not only of income, but of health and lifespan.

Within the rich countries, the prevailing scholarly view has been one of inter-generational 'persistent inequality', after a landmark study with that title (Shavit and Blossfeld 1993). Ever ongoing scholarly revision has recently turned this picture in a somewhat more positive direction. The distribution of educational resources seems to have become less unequal over the past two generations (Breen et al. 2009).

In the gendering of educational resources there has been a silent revolution, with women clearly overtaking men in educational enrolment in Argentina, Brazil and Malaysia, as well as in the most developed countries of the world. Women are now doing as well as men, or slightly better, in countries like Bangladesh, China,

Iran (!) and Mexico, but not (yet) in India, Indonesia or Vietnam (UNDP 2007: table 28).

Power resources: Democratization and its limits

Human actors can also use politics as a resource to obtain their goals, i.e., in a collective organization of power or pressure. On the whole, modern history has meant an equalization of power resources, within nations particularly. But it has been an extremely drawn-out process, and one not yet globally completed.

Democratization was not an inexorable evolution of modernity, but rather a historical drama, concentrated, in the rich world, around the two World Wars (Therborn 1977), and in the ex-Colonial Zone around decolonization and its vicissitudes. The simple principle of governments deriving from universal suffrage is not yet a universal human right, and is still denied in Saudi Arabia. It took two centuries for it to be recognized all over the United States, until the late 1960s when Southern African Americans finally could vote. For the Brazilian republic it took one century, until 1988, when the large numbers of illiterates were finally accepted as political citizens. Only in 1994 was it endorsed in South Africa.

Modern political history has not been only meandering paths to democracy, but very much also the rise of dictatorships. Modern dictatorships are not based on socioeconomic exclusion, but on a de facto monopolization of power, by hierarchical institutions, the state administration and its security apparatus, the military, or the ruling party. In the twentieth century, they played a major role. But the century ended with a series of dictatorship defeats – some linked, others not. The major wave of Latin American democratization in the 1980s was mainly driven by national developments. Brazil was on a path of opening from above, pushed by

the labour movement of São Paolo and the Catholic
Church. The Argentine military was devastated by its
defeat in the Malvinas/Falklands War. The clever Chilean
dictatorship lost a crucial referendum, which the regime
was then too divided to reverse. In Central America, it
turned out that the insurgency against horrendous inequalities could neither be crushed nor win, leading on
to peace deals of democracy. In South Korea, fearless
street struggles of students and industrial workers, supported by large sections of the middle class, wrested
democratization from the military, bereft of its assassi-
nated long-time leader, Park Chung-hee. The outra-
geously blood-stained, but skilfully managed, Indonesian
military dictatorship, with between half a million and 1
million people killed in a few months of 1965–6, was
ousted by popular protests in the wake of the East Asian
financial crisis of 1997–8.

The implosion of Eastern European Communism
issued into a democratization of political resources
along the East-Central strip of Europe, from the Baltics
to Bulgaria, and later processes of a similar kind in the
Ukraine and Georgia. It also ended the infatuation with
one-party states in several countries of Africa. In Russia,
in Central Asia, in Belarus, and in most of the Caucasus,
however, it mainly meant substituting one kind of power
inequality for another.

Surviving one-party states are currently engaged
in gradual de-hierarchization and inclusive de-
monopolization, in China, Cuba and Vietnam, though
not in dynastic North Korea.

The inter-national political trajectory has also been
uneven, with the rise of world empires – first the British
and then the American, above all – and of Cold War
'superpowers', for a long time trumping the emergence
of the League of Nations and of the United Nations.
Nevertheless, the votes of the UN General Assembly
do increasingly indicate a somewhat less unequal

distribution of inter-national political influence. On issues relating to Palestine, the USA is regularly outvoted, but without effect on the heavily armed Zionist ground. And the Anglo-French competition for the votes of the Security Council in 2003 about a US-led attack on Iraq meant nothing in the end. Votes may count, but when ruling elite interests are at stake, guns decide.

Within nations, social movements, collective associations and wide-franchised elections – democratization, in short – have brought about a major equalization of political resources, once monopolized by monarchs and other despots. But, as with economic resources, political equalization has been stopped or reversed recently, by de-unionization, political party erosion, and general social dissolution of the popular classes. A difference from what has happened to economic resources, which are ever more concentrated, has been the rise of electronic social media and their possibilities of self-generated mass communication. In the protest movements of 2011, the Arab Spring, the pan-Mediterranean revolts, and the North Atlantic Occupy movements, we saw their power of mobilization – but also the limits of their potential for social transformation.

IV

Today's Unequal World

My inclination to see the present as history has already taken us up to the present, and we encountered current experiences of death and stunting already in the first chapter. Here we shall look into some systematic patterns in today's unequal world. And we shall try to answer three great puzzles about how we got here.

7

Current World Patterns and Dynamics of Inequalities

Unequal Developments among the Unequals

The United Nations Development Programme has recently begun adjusting its Human Development Indices[13] to take into account the inequality of development. They broaden the income picture above by including the resource of education and a measure of vital inequality. On the whole, the UNDP finds that about a quarter of human development in the world is lost due to unequal distributions. While the size of this estimate may be open to dispute, the UNDP efforts make it possible to compare different kinds of inequality across the world (see table 8).

The different kinds of inequality are unevenly distributed across the world. Vital inequality, in spite of its class resilience even in the developed welfare states, is

[13] The Human Development Index is a composite index of life expectancy, education and per capita national income.

Table 8   *The loss of human well-being due to different kinds of inequality in 2011 in the regions of the world.* Percentage loss of Human Development Index value.

	Overall index	Life expectancy	Education	Income
Very highly developed	11.5	5.2	6.2	22.2
Least developed	32.4	34.7	36.8	25.3
Arab states	28.4	18.0	40.8	17.8
East Asia	21.3	14.3	21.9	26.8
Eastern Europe, Central Asia	12.7	11.7	10.7	15.7
Latin America	26.1	13.4	23.2	39.3
South Asia	28.4	26.9	40.9	15.1
Sub-S. Africa	34.5	39.0	35.8	28.4
World	23.0	19.0	26.2	23.4

Source: UNDP (2011: table 3)

creating most havoc in Africa, and generally in the least developed world. Unequal education is particularly striking in India, as with the rest of South Asia, and in the Arab states. China fares much better than India, because of smaller inequalities of life expectancy and of education, losing 22 per cent of its index value overall as against an Indian loss of 28. Latin American inequality is concentrated on income, in spite of a decade of equalization.

On a world scale, the rich, or 'highly developed', countries are the least unequal. Among the richest countries, the USA loses most of its development to inequality: 15 per cent overall, as compared to 7 per cent in Germany, 8 per cent in the UK, and 9 per cent in France and Spain. The least losses were recorded in Scandinavia and in Slovenia, at somewhat below 6 per cent. Closest to the USA in overall inequality is Southern Europe, from Portugal to Greece losing 10–13 per cent of its Human Development Index value to inequality. Adjusted for distribution, US development is slightly below that of Italy. Japanese data are missing, but South Korea comes out somewhat worse than the USA, due to the most unequal educational distribution among developed countries, which seems to be largely a generational effect, caused by a recent enormous expansion of higher education.

In Ibero-America, the worst losses were recorded in Bolivia and Colombia – a third of the Development Index – due mainly to enduring income inequality. But it is worth noticing that the region's extremely unequal income distribution coexists with considerably less inequality of life expectancy and education. In the most unequal countries, Haiti and several African countries, from Namibia to the Central African Republic, a good 40 per cent of the already low average development level is lost to inequality.

Internal national differences in human development are huge. For example, the ratio between the Human Development Index (HDI) of the richest and of the poorest quintile in India (in 1997–9) is about the same as that of the national US HDI to the national Indian HDI in 2011. According to the estimates of Michael Grimm et al. (2009: table 1), the level of human development enjoyed by the richest fifth of the people in poor countries like Kyrgyzstan, Vietnam, Indonesia and Bolivia is on a par with, or higher than, that allocated to the poorest fifth of the United States. In Brazil, 60 per cent of the population live on a higher level than the poorest fifth of Americans (data refer to *circa* 2000). The figures of Grimm et al. are empirically derived estimates, produced with great scholarly ingenuity, but should be taken as indicators, rather than demonstrated truths. Following UNDP methodology, these estimates discount increases of income, which means giving more weight to health and education. But they do highlight a very important aspect of contemporary world inequality, often obscured by GDP-focused comparisons: intranational inequalities can be stunningly wide.

Life expectancy differentials illustrate this very well. Around 2010, the lives of Swedish males in the upper-middle-class municipality of Danderyd (a suburb of Stockholm) were on average 8.6 years longer than those of fellow citizens in the far north, working-class and small peasant municipality of Pajala (Statistics Sweden 2011). That is slightly more than the national difference between Sweden and Egypt (UNDP 2011: table 1). In the UK, the life-gaps are even larger, as we noticed for London above and as we shall see further below.

The UNDP does not estimate existential inequality, but it does have a gender inequality index: a composite index of maternal mortality and adolescent fertility, secondly of secondary education and parliamentary seats in comparison with males, and thirdly of relative labour force participation rates. Viewed in this way, current

Table 9   *Gender inequality in the world, 2011*
Inequality Index.

Country groups & countries	
Very high development	0.224
Least developed	0.594
Most egalitarian (Sweden)	0.049
Arab States	0.563
China	0.209
USA	0.299
Eastern Europe & Central Asia	0.311
Latin America & the Caribbean	0.445
South Asia	0.601
Sub-Saharan Africa	0.610
World	0.492

Source: UNDP (2011: table 4)

gender inequality in the world looks like table 9: the lower the index, the lower is inequality.

Composite indices are always open to debate about the selection and weighting of indicators, and the UNDP index appears to be giving more weight to gendered reproductive health than to existential gendering. The reason why the USA comes out so badly, and more gender unequal than China, seems to be due primarily to maternal mortality and adolescent births, which also explain why the UK has the same index value as China. Korea and Japan score low, together with continental Western Europe, with index numbers around 0.10–0.12, while Switzerland, Germany and Scandinavia stay below 0.1. In South Asia, India is more unequal than both Pakistan and Bangladesh, in spite of less maternal mortality, having more teenage fertility, less female parliamentary representation, and more gender-skewed secondary education and labour force participation than Bangladesh. The worst sinners against gender equality, according to the UNDP calculations, with values above 0.7, are the African Sahel countries, Chad, Mali, Niger and, further, Congo-Kinshasa, Afghanistan and Yemen. Two sub-Saharan African countries are somewhat better than the world average, Rwanda and Burundi, while South Africa stands on the world meridian.

Existential gender inequality may also be approached by investigating family norms and practices, as I have done in a historical study of sex and power in the twentieth century (Therborn 2004). Today the world's two major redoubts of male family power are sub-Saharan Africa and South Asia, in both cases particularly their northern parts. According to survey data reported by UNICEF (2007: 19–20), in countries like Nigeria and Mali about two-thirds of wives say husbands alone make decisions on daily household expenditure, and alone decide whether the wife can visit a friend or a relative. In Uganda and Tanzania, this is reported by just under half of all wives, in Kenya and Ghana by about a third of all married women, down to a fifth in Zimbabwe. (South Africa was not part of the survey.) In Bangladesh, corresponding conditions are experienced by a third of women; in Morocco and Egypt by a good quarter. (The Indian survey worded its questions somewhat differently, but only a third of married Indian women said they could go alone to the market, to a health facility, and outside the community. In 2005–6, 45 per cent of Indian women aged 15–49 agreed that there was at least one specific reason for which a husband was right in beating his wife (Namasivayam et al. 2012: table 2).

Under UN auspices and domestic Feminist pressures, laws bolstering patriarchal power were scrapped in Western Europe and the Americas in the last third of the twentieth century (Therborn 2004: 100ff.). While not without influence on official norms, this global process had a much more limited impact in Africa and Asia. Arab countries, and many African countries, e.g. Congo-Kinshasa, have laws of wifely obedience and requirements of husband / father / male relative consent, for a passport for example (Banda 2008: 83ff.). A Mali government bill repealing the obedience clause was withdrawn in 2009 after conservative male opposition, although it had been passed by parliament (www.WLUML.org/news/mali-womens-rights).

One area where resurgent patriarchy and masculinism can be measured is in the sexual ratio of births, of surviving children, and of male–female life expectancy. Low fertility – an enforced public policy in China and a chosen option in other parts of the world – patriarchal/masculinist son preference, and prenatal scanning technology have recently skewed sex ratios of births in a distinctive set of countries. They have been spotted in South Asia, South Korea, China, Vietnam, in the Caucasian republics of Armenia, Azerbaijan and Georgia, and in the western Balkans of Albania and Montenegro (UNFPA 2011).

In India, the sex ratio of 0- to 6-year-olds has increased from a normal distribution of l04–6 boys per 100 girls in 1981 and 1991, to 109:100 in 2011 (UNFPA 2011: 15ff.). The masculinist push has been strongest in post-Maoist China, soaring to a sex ratio at birth of 120:100 in 2005, and so far stabilizing there, up from 107:100 in 1982 (UNFPA 2011: 13).

Marriages arranged by fathers and/or mothers remain important in the twenty-first century, although their exact prevalence is unknown. Such marriages are still predominant in South Asia, i.e., in India, Pakistan, Nepal and Bangladesh (Mody 2008; WLUML 2006: ch. 3; Jones 2010), a practice carried into the current diaspora (Charsley and Shaw 2006). It is widespread in rural Central Asia, in West Asia, including rural Turkey, and north Africa, and in sub-Saharan Africa. It is occurring in substantial parts of Southeast Asia, such as Malaysia and Indonesia, backed up by permissive national or provincial law (WLUML 2006: ch. 3). Islamic law forbids forced marriages, but no active consent is required of the bride. Parental marriage arrangements remain important in China, particularly in the rural west (Xu et al. 2007; Judd 2010).

However, it is important to underline the contemporary inadequacy of the binary conception of arranged marriages and marriages of choice. Classical arranged marriages without the future spouses – or at least the bride – being consulted, have largely disappeared in East Asia (Jones 2010; Tsutsui 2010; Zang 2008), and are eroding in the other parts of Asia as well (WLUML 2006; Bhandari forthcoming). In Arab countries such as Egypt and Morocco, there is overwhelming support for the idea that women should have a right to choose their spouse, and also an overwhelming perception that this is currently the case (UNDP 2005: 263–4). Between exclusive parental arrangement and individual choice without asking your parents, there is now a crowded Afro-Asian continuum of initiatives, vetoes, negotiations, accommodations and compromises. But marriage in Africa and Asia remains a family, rather than an individual, affair.

Racism and ethnic stigmatization is the other main manifestation of existential inequality. Above, we noticed that major egalitarian existential advances were made in the second half, and particularly in the last third, of the past century, culminating in the early 1990s with the fall of apartheid in South Africa. Since then, however, it seems that the forward march of human existential equality has been stopped – except for in the Andean countries of South America where indigenous peoples are asserting themselves, and regarding homosexuality and same-sex marriages in Western Europe and the Americas – in some places it has even been forced to retreat. In a number of countries, previous inter-ethnic and -religious *modi vivendi* have broken up along with the carapace of authoritarian regimes under which coexistence was secured. The wars of Yugoslav and of Caucasian post-Communist succession are the most dramatic examples; the 1994 Rwandan genocide while the UN was literally looking on, the most horrendous. But examples abound, from violent post-Communist Russian racism against Caucasians and Central Asians, to mounting anti-Semitism in Hungary and Poland, vicious discrimination against Sinti and Roma in Slovakia, Hungary and Romania, violent sectarian conflicts in post-invasion Iraq, ghastly discrimination against the Rohingya in Myanmar, etc., etc. A master race self-conception among Jews is getting increasingly stronger in Israel, with accelerated colonization of Palestinian land and increasingly vociferous demands for the deportation – 'transfer' – of Palestinians from Palestine.

Nevertheless, in spite of some setbacks and some new ugly displays of denial of human existential equality, the late twentieth-century achievements of Feminism and of anti-racist movements are not in visible danger of being undone. And three categories of people have recently gained recognition and respect for the first time in the modern era: indigenous peoples, the extra-moderns; secondly, homosexuals, the outlaws of modern sexuality; and thirdly, people with disabilities, previously the hidden people.

Vital inequality, on the other hand, is increasing within rich nations, as we took note of both in the first chapter and in the historical overview above. Inter-country inequality turned into increase around 1990, because of AIDS in Africa and the restoration of capitalism in the former Soviet Union. In both cases, a certain alleviation of the death toll has been noticed in recent years – in South Africa, since 2005. Nevertheless, by 2010, 10 per cent extra of the Russian male and 14 per cent of the Ukrainian male population who survived until the age of 15 are dying before the age of 60, compared to the death rate of 1990. For males, capitalism in the Ukraine has been almost as lethal as AIDS in South Africa, where the death rate climbed an extra 15 per cent. Among women, the post-Communist hecatomb is smaller, about 4 per cent more dying before 60, and much smaller than the AIDS toll in South Africa. During the same period, premature adult deaths in the UK decreased by 4 per cent for men and 2 per cent for women (Rajaratnam 2010: 1710–11).

Vital inequality is also leaving a dramatic imprint on city life, as we noticed above in the historical overview with respect to London. Among the local authorities of London, life in the poorest authority was 5 years shorter than in the richest at the beginning of New Labour reign (in 1999–2001), and almost 9 years (8.9) shorter towards the end of it (2006–8) (London Health

Observatory 2011). The London boroughs' gap in life expectancy is equal to that between UK and Guatemala (UNICEF 2012: table 1). The extreme life-gap between Glasgow Calton and Glasgow Lenzie – 28 years – is the same as that between the UK and Haiti. The rather central neighbourhood of Calton, by no means a slum, is an extreme case of still unclear provenance, though interwoven with unemployment and abuse of drugs and alcohol, visible even to a casual visitor (for data and context, see Hanlon et al. 2008). But bad neighbourhood environments seem to have their own negative effects on people's health independent of individual deprivations (Bilger and Carrien 2013). On a larger area level, the life expectancy gap between Glasgow and Chelsea–Kensington, 12 years in 2009–10 (ONS 2011), is the same as the gulf between the UK and the Ukraine (WHO 2012: table 1).

The World's Pattern of Income Inequality

Income distribution tables have to be seen like political opinion polls: interesting; indispensable for the really interested; usually getting the main proportions right, but not always the top winner or the close loser; always varying from one source to the next; and tagged with margins of error. In contrast to opinion polls, on income distribution there are no final electoral results, deciding whose estimate was wrong and whose correct.

Estimates of national distribution are nowadays based on household surveys, with similar margins of error to political polls, although the economic surveys are usually much larger. They have always great difficulties in getting at the very rich, and often the very poor. This is routinely dealt with by 'censoring', i.e., by simply stopping counting and estimating incomes above and below a certain amount. The actual amount of inequality is correspondingly censored.

International comparisons are also dogged with some basic difficulties of comparability. While most national surveys are income surveys, many Asian nations – including big ones like India, Pakistan, Bangladesh and Indonesia – stick to surveys of consumer expenditure. While usually presented together in the same UN or World Bank table, sometimes without a footnote, income and consumption give very different estimates of inequality. As the rich save more, and the poor often have to consume via debt, consumer expenditure gives substantially lower figures of inequality. How much they vary has never been standardized, but it seems to be in the range of 6–10 Gini points. A lesser problem, so far, has been that OECD data usually refer to disposable income, after taxes and public transfers, whereas other income surveys usually refer to gross market income. As there is not much public redistribution going on outside the developed OECD countries, the effect of this discrepancy is rather minor.

At least among European scholars, the Luxemburg Income Study (LIS), run by an international scholarly consortium and based in Luxemburg, has been considered the best source of comparable intra-national income inequality, based as it is on standardized national surveys. It probably still is, but it does not have the validity of an electoral outcome. This dawned upon me rather dramatically upon discovering the huge difference in US inequality as reported by the LIS and by the Congressional Budget Office. According to the former, the American Gini coefficient of disposable income was 0.38 in 2007 (LIS 2012), while according to the latter it was 0.49 (after transfers and federal taxes) (CBO 2011a: 19). The UNDP (2011: table 3) put the figure at 0.41, which may or may not have taken state and local taxes also into consideration (please note that the coefficient is sometimes, as in table 10, multiplied by 100, then ranging between 0 and 100, instead of 0 and 1).

Absolute figures of distribution, then, are not to be trusted, and mathematical modelling on the basis of them is risky. But any knownothing-ism is unwarranted. While some important inter-country comparisons are tricky, the contours of the world pattern are rather clear and scholarly uncontroversial (table 10).

Alas, I cannot claim that table 10 is *the* true picture of national income inequality in the world, but I do think that it is, at least at the moment of writing, the most accurate picture available, based mainly on national monographs and official reports and on data collections from resourceful regional institutions in Africa, Asia, Europe and Latin America. In comparison with many respectable mainstream databases, the Luxemburg Income Study, Eurostat, the OECD, the UNDP and the World Bank, it involves some major revisions. Most important, given the global weight of the item, is the very significant push upwards for US inequality figures, derived directly from the Budget Office of the US Congress. In spite of all the efforts of parts of the UK top floors of politics and finance, the Atlantic divide of economic inequality has widened. (The UK Office of National Statistics has been checked.) The frequent international under-reporting of Indian inequality by confounding consumption expenditure and income is corrected on the basis of two different, but concurring, national studies. The Netherlands and Scandinavia, and Sweden in particular, have an inflated equality record in international media, altered above after checking official national statistical sources.

The relative order of China and India remains unsettled. A Chinese expenditure survey used by the Asian Development Bank (2012b: ch. 2) supported the usual view of lesser Indian inequality. The urban–rural gap is undoubtedly much larger in China, by far the widest in

Table 10   *Income inequality in countries of the world,*
2005–2011
Gini coefficients and quintile ratios, i.e., the ratio of the
income share of the most affluent fifth of the population to
that of the poorest.

Top inequality	Gini above 60	Quintile ratio
South Africa (2008)	66	55
Namibia (2004)	64	
Very high inequality	*Gini clearly > 50*	*Quintile ratios > 20*
Brazil (2011) & Bolivia, Colombia, Dom. Rep., Guatemala, Honduras	56	22
High inequality	*Gini around 50*	*Quintile ratios > 10*
China	49–54	12
India, & a few countries of Asia, e.g. Malaysia, Thailand	54–55	...
Zambia & parts of Africa, incl. Nigeria	55 / 49	15 / ...
Argentina (urban 2011)	49	15
Mexico (2010) & most remaining parts of Latin America	48	13
Very substantial inequality	*Gini in the 40s*	*Quintile ratios > 7*
USA (2007)	49	7.6
Russia	42	8
Substantial inequality	*Gini in the 30s*	*Quintile ratios ≥ 4*
Spain	34	6.8
UK	33	5.3
Japan	33	6
South Korea	32	6
Poland	31	5.0
France	31	4.6
Ethiopia	30	4
Germany	29	4.5

Table 10 *Continued*

Sweden	30	4.5
Denmark	28	4.4
Finland	29	5.3
Delimited in equality	*Gini < 30*	*Quintile ratio < 4*
Austria	26	3.8
Czech Republic	25	3.5
Netherlands	29	. . .
Norway	25	3.6
Slovakia	26	3.8
Slovenia	24	3.5

Sources: Africa: African Statistical Yearbook (2012: 73); South Africa: Leibbrandt et al. (2010: tables 2.9 and A.2.3); China: Li Shi et al. (2011); India: Das (2012: 61), referring to overall wage inequality, with a Gini of 55, and World Bank economists Peter Lanjouw and Rinku Murgai reported in *The Economist* (2012: 8); Japan and South Korea: OECD (2011b: table A.1.1); other Asia: Asian Development Bank (2012a: table2.1);
EU: Eurostat (2013)];
Latin America: CEPAL (2012: tables II.A.1-2);
Nordic countries and the Netherlands – national statistical bureaux:
Denmark: Danmarks Statistik (2011)
Finland: Official Statistics of Finland (2012)
Netherlands (Gini only): Central Bureau of Statistics (2012)
Norway: Statistisk sentralbyrå (2012)
Sweden: Statistics Sweden (2013c);
for the rest of Europe and Russia: UNDP (2011: table 3).

Asia, while state/provincial differences have become larger in India. The richest 5 and 1 per cent seem to take a larger share of the national total in India than in China (table 7 above). The place of Indonesia, close to China and India, is also unclear. The Asian Development Bank puts it in between them. Bangladesh and Pakistan appear less income-unequal than India (Asian Development Bank 2012b: 47ff., 68ff.; Atkinson et al. 2010: 730ff.).

The weight of history lies very unevenly on the world picture above, which, taken as a whole, vindicates the potential of contemporary political economy. Communist equalization has been discarded in China and in Russia, but seems to have survived in Czecho-Slovakia and Slovenia, with less stark pre-Communist inequality. Capitalist as well as pre-capitalist inequality, on the other hand, still holds down Latin America, South Africa and India, in spite of many honourable attempts at change.

National economic inequality in the world exhibits some clear historical geo-economic patterns. Worst-off are the former White racist settler-*cum*-mining-and/or-plantation countries, South Africa and Namibia, Brazil and Bolivia, and most of Latin America. Sub-Saharan Africa as a whole has a very varied pattern of distribution. Ranked next to the unfortunate heirs of apartheid are similar socioeconomically little-developed mineral-rich countries run by small rent-appropriating elites, like the Central African Republic and Angola. Then there is a group of dynamic, hierarchical and corrupt economies – some with mineral resources, like Nigeria and Zambia; some not, like Kenya. At an early stage of modern economic development and without extractive booty to offer are countries with, so far, limited economic inequality, such as Ethiopia (currently growing rapidly) and the Sahel countries.

Latin America is more homogeneously unequal. Only one single country today has a Gini coefficient below 40 – *chavista* Venezuela, just barely. Late twentieth-century neoliberalism pushed the historically least unequal countries, Costa Rica and Uruguay, above that bar. The never-ending tragedies of Haiti, which go back to the traumatic vengeance of imperial France and the USA against the world's first Black revolution, make a special case. But continental Latin inequality derives from an interconnected and overlapping constellation

of powerful forces of inequality: huge mine rents, plantation slavery, fertile *latifundia* and their land rents with
or without (Argentina, Uruguay) Indian serfs, and racial
hierarchies. Processes of continuously expanded reproduction of inequality were occasionally derailed by
revolutions, as in Mexico and Bolivia, or by Presidential
populism, but never for very long, and were then
enforced anew by Cold War gusts from the North, and
later by stern neoliberal sermons from the 'Washington
Consensus'.

The Northeast Asian pioneers of successful extra-
European development, Japan, Korea and Taiwan have
an economic distribution strikingly similar to that of the
European welfare states. The Northeast Asian developmental states have kept the worst economic inequality
at bay, more through promoting patriarchal and ethnic
social cohesion than by redistribution policies. Korea
has the lowest income inequality among prime-age
adults in the OECD area, and even current Japan is
slightly below the average in this respect (OECD 2011a:
figure 6.1). In the big Asian economies of China, India,
Indonesia and Bangladesh, economic inequality has
risen strongly in the last two decades (Asian Development Bank 2012a: 7), but 'developing Asia' remains
below the inequality arcs of Africa and Latin America.

Europe is holding tightly together, at least for the time
being. No country west of Russia has a Gini at or above
40. Overall EU Gini is 31 with a 80:20[14] ratio of 5.
Western European economic inequality is headed by
Spain, Portugal, the UK and Greece. North-Central
Europe is the least unequal part of the world, most
reliably represented by Norway, despite its oil rent.

---

[14] This is the ratio between the income of people at the (affluent) 80th percentile of the population and that of the people
at the (poor) 20th percentile.

The legacy is still there in the social states, now under liberal siege, of the uniquely influential European labour movement, with its different currents, Social Democracy, Christian Democracy and Communism.

Children's Opportunities: Inter-generational Income Relations

The new economics of inequality of opportunity is opening up a new vista compared to the twentieth-century sociological preoccupation with inter-generational social mobility. The concern is the same, the liberal idea of equality of opportunity, but the economists are looking into broader foci of outcomes, not primarily occupations but earnings, health and educational achievements – the latter also covered by the sociology of education. Whereas the main message of mobility research was the commonality of industrial societies (Eriksson and Goldthorpe 1992), current inequality of opportunity research is highlighting inter-national differences of opportunity.

The career earnings of adult children depend significantly on the income, and also the education, of their parents. But the inequality of opportunity, or what economists call the generational elasticity of income, varies strongly between countries (table 8). The measure of elasticity can take values between 0 and 1, at 0 meaning that none of the parental income differentials is transmitted to their children as adults, and at 1 that all of it is.

The overall picture in table 11 is confirmed by several similar studies, with somewhat different methodologies and databases, referring to adult income in the 1990s or 2000s, and to the former income of the parents of those adults (e.g. OECD 2008: ch. 8; Marrero and Rodríguez 2012; Lefranc et al. 2008; Jäntti et al. 2006).

Table 11 *Inequality of income opportunity by the end of the twentieth century*
Elasticity coefficients: the higher the coefficient, the stronger the link between generational incomes, and the more inequality of opportunity.

UK	0.50
Italy	0.50
US	0.47
France	0.41
Spain	0.40
Japan	0.34
Germany	0.32
Sweden	0.27
Australia	0.26
Canada	0.25
Finland	0.18
Norway	0.17
Denmark	0.15

Source: Corak (2012: table 1)

Most noteworthy, given widespread ideological perceptions, is the limited equality of opportunity in the US, the discrepancy being primarily due to an extraordinary inappropriateness of the rags-to-riches fairy tale. The children of the poorest fifth of the American population are much more likely to get stuck at the low end of the income hierarchy, clearly more so than even in the UK (OECD 2008: table 8.1). Nor should it go unnoticed that inequality of opportunity is positively correlated with inequality of outcome: the countries with the highest intra-generation inequality have the highest inter-generational inequality, and the lowest inter-generation inequality is found among the countries with the lowest intra-generational inequality of outcome.

However, one should always be careful before totally dismissing popular ideologies. Usually, they became powerful because they once had some touch with reality.

The relatively high income mobility in Australia and Canada, both more unequal overall than continental Northwestern Europe, does indicate the possibility of an independent inequality of opportunity dimension, which the USA might once have had and has now lost.

There is also a growing number of multi-generational studies. One of the most representative is a Swedish study following up a study of school children in the 1930s in the middle-sized city of Malmö, expanding it into four generations for education and three for earnings. A third of the grandchildren (born around 1981) whose grandfathers (born around 1896) were in the top quintile of earnings were themselves in the top bracket. The risk of being stuck among the bottom fifth was much smaller, and the educational association, though statistically significant, was weak (Lindahl et al. 2012).

For the rest of the world, information is scanty. But what we have tends to support the strong link between what influential ideologies want to separate: opportunity and outcome. Very outcome-inegalitarian Brazil has also much less equality of opportunity than the US and the UK, referring to the birth cohorts of 1960 (Milburn et al. 2009: 37). An Indian study (Singh 2012), comparing its own results with others, finds intergenerational relations of earnings (and consumption) more unequal in India than in Europe, but much less so than in Latin America. Deng et al. (2012) found more inequality of opportunity in urban China than in Europe or Canada, but without a possibility of a precise comparison with the USA or Brazil.

The Current Dynamics of Income Inequality – At the Top and at the Bottom

The '1 vs 99 per cent' is originally an American debate, launched by Nobel Laureate Joseph Stiglitz in the spring of 2011, based on American findings. According to the US Congressional Budget Office (CBO) (2011a: table 2), the top 1 per cent of income earners more than doubled their appropriation of national disposable income, after transfers and federal taxes, between 1979 and 2007. The next richest 19 per cent basically kept their share – about 36 per cent – whereas all others, from the poor to the middle class, lost.

Who are the American 1 per cent? Non-financial executives and managers make up 31 per cent; medical professionals (doctors) – the classical enemies of 'socialized medicine' – constitute 16 per cent; financial professionals 14 per cent (a doubling from 1979); and lawyers 8 per cent (CBO 2011a: 18). Among the richest 0.1 per cent, three-quarters are in business, non-financial executives comprise 41 per cent, financial ones 18, other businessmen 14, professionals of law and medicine 11, computing and other technical professionals and scientists 4. Stars of the arts, media and sport add up to 3 per cent only (Hacker and Pierson 2010: 46).

Apart from the expected power and wealth of business executives, outside as well as inside finance, what is striking here is the income-generating power of the American professions. One example is the average annual remuneration of psychiatrists, $216,500 in 2010, compared to that of a Harvard professor, $193,800. A law partner can make more than a million dollars, but all pale, of course, in comparison with corporate CEOs, from around $20 million upwards (Hacker 2012: table B).

As we saw above in table 7, the recent income appropriation of the top US 1 per cent is unique in the world in its acceleration, although a few Latin American and African countries can probably compete in terms of the absolute share of national income But there has been a fairly general tendency in the OECD countries for the top income earners to run ahead. In terms of household income (which depends also on gender relations and household composition), Sweden had in fact the largest gap in income development between the top and the bottom 10 per cent, at 2 percentage points annually from the mid-1980s to the mid-2000s, compared to 1.6 per cent a year in the UK and 1.4 per cent in the US. The most affluent 10 per cent of the households kept the same edge over the population as a whole in Sweden and in the USA, appropriating 0.6 percentage points more every year, as against 0.4 in the UK (OECD 2011a: table 1).

There are also good reasons to look out for the dynamics at the bottom. Here again, the US stands out in the developed world. From 1980 to 2005, real earnings for the lowest-paid 40 per cent of full-time working men declined on average each year of the quarter-century (OECD 2008: figure 3.3). Only in Canada did anything similar occur. But the lowest decile of men did have a fall in real earnings also in Germany, the Netherlands, Norway and Sweden (OECD 2011a: figure 5.4). In the decade from the mid-1990s to the mid-2000s, the real income of the poorest quintile of the population declined in Austria, Germany, Japan, Mexico and Turkey, as well as in the US (OECD 2008: 287).

For the twenty years from the mid-1980s to the mid-2000s, all developed countries, with the single exception of Greece, experienced an increase in income inequality, albeit of different sizes and period timing (OECD 2011a: table 1). Developing Asia – apart from Central Asia, recovering, at least in part, from their post-Communist crisis – has had the same experience, with some minor exceptions in Pakistan, the Philippines and Thailand (ADB 2012b: table 2.2.1). This points to some general factors of contemporary developed capitalism at work, while the US extremism just noticed above highlights the necessity of paying attention to national variability. The ample and heated scholarly discussion has not arrived at any conclusive consensus. It has centred around three clusters of variables: globalization, technology and politics. Some arguments seem to turn out to be more tenable than others (OECD 2011a: table 2).

For the rich OECD world and its recent inequality rises, it seems that 'globalization', of trade openings and foreign investment, has not played a major role. Migration, a third important aspect of contemporary world connectivity, is not included in the OECD calculations. It is most probably not a major general factor, but, in the form of very substantial increase of immigration from the poor world from 1970, it may well have added downward pressure on the lower end of US employment, but hardly a crucial one, as the explosion of US inequality took place in the 1980s, after the initial wave of new immigration and before the flood of the 1990s (cf. Mishel et al. 2009: 195ff.; Congressional Budget Office 2011b: 12).

Technology is another contender for the prize of explaining the growth of inequality, and apparently the predominant one in mainstream economics. The new, electronic 'information age' has increased the demand for and the productivity of skilled labour, while diminishing the demand for the semi-skilled. The result is a polarized labour market development, with a growing share of high-skilled, well-paid jobs, as well as of low-paid, precarious jobs as servants to the former 'creative' class, while middle-range blue- and white-collar occupations decline. Empirical evidence shows the truth of such a current tendency towards labour market polarization. Erik Olin Wright (Wright and Rogers 2011: 160f.) and others have found it in the US, and it has been discovered with respect to the whole EU labour market for 1993–2006 – pronounced in Germany and the UK, and not applicable to France, which had an overall upgrading of its labour market (Goos et al. 2009: table 2). In the USA in particular, pay differentials by educational level increased strongly after 1979 – in the 1980s, in particular (Congressional Budget Office 2011b: 8).

Radical social scientists have put an emphasis on politics, on political alterations to the market game, and on the anti-trade union offensive – by some governments as well as by employers – in particular. The official OECD (2011a: table 2) study largely proves them right. Deregulation of product markets, reducing employee protection and lowering unemployment benefits are all significantly correlated with increasing wage inequality, which is much aggravated by widening employer options for precarious temporary and part-time employment (OECD 2011a: 32ff.). The decline of unions is found both by the OECD and by a recent American sociological study by Volscho and Kelly (2012: figure 2), arguing, by standard socioeconomic modelling, that the increased appropriation of the top 1 per cent is largely caused by trade union decline.

With due respect to all the research done along the lines of globalization, technology and politics, from which I personally have learnt so much, I think they all have significant limitations. The OECD conceptualization of globalization is too narrow to capture recent changes in the planetary economy. The technology-skill demand view appears too bland to capture the extreme polarization of some recent inequality developments (cf. Mishel et al. 2013). The political argument has not (yet) provided any plausible causal path from, e.g., union decline to soaring Wall Street income (cf. Kaplan and Rauh 2007: 6).

As a 'conjecture', in the sense of Simon Kuznets, I am going to argue that an analytical study of the recent drive to ever-increasing income inequality in the rich nations should pinpoint the immediate dynamics at the top and at the bottom, and then try to relate them to the current world dynamics of capitalism.

Table 12   *Capital managed by the top 50 firms in the US securities industry, 1972–2004*

	$ millions
1972	2,768
1987	29,636
2004	696,087

Source: Kaplan and Rauh (2007: table 2c)

Top incomes are driven by capital income, not *rentier* income as 100 years ago, but managed capital income – of fund managers of capital pools, of business executives remunerated with stocks – and by capital investments topping up upper-middle-class incomes. The explosion of pooled capital under asset management is really staggering. Just a few US examples appear in table 12.

The 'securities industry' is, by and large, what laymen would call 'investment banking': Goldman Sachs and company. Hedge funds constitute another branch of pooled managed capital. In 1986, these funds managed $20 billion, in 2004, $934 billion (Kaplan and Rauh 2007: table 3a). Non-financial firms have grown too, including top law firms increasing their revenues six-fold between 1984 and 2004 (Kaplan and Rauh 2007: 40).

In contrast to the business economists who have gathered the data above, I cannot see how their figures provide any support for the idea of 'skill-biased technological change', but they certainly do for the 'greater scale' of capital.

To the US experience, we might add an example from Sweden, often seen as an ideal country by long-suffering Anglo-Saxon egalitarians. In spite of currently sliding backwards, Sweden is still a significantly less indecent country than most in the rich OECD world. But from a relatively low base of income inequality, Sweden, as we have noticed above, has had since the 1990s a vigorous development of inequality, the Gini coefficient increasing by 9 points from 1980 to 2008 (Björklund and Jäntti 2011:42), not so far behind the US increase, from 1979 to 2007, of 12 points (Congressional Budget Office 2011a: 19). The driving force in the Swedish case has been capital income, which makes up a third of the income of the top 10 per cent, while only 7 per cent for the next decile (Statistics Sweden 2010: table 39).

With the help of Simone Scarpa, a graduate student at Linnaeus University, Sweden, who has made the calculations from the LISA database of Statistics Sweden, I have looked at the income development for 1991–2010 of the Stockholm Metropolitan area. In the period, the less affluent 80 per cent of the population saw their income share decline, while the most prosperous 10 per cent had their share augmented from 25 to 32 per cent. The labour earnings of the latter increased, while those of the four lowest-paid deciles declined in absolute terms. But what decided the privilege of the top 10 per cent was capital income. This increased for them by 282 per cent over the period, while it actually *declined* for deciles nine to seven, and for the poorest four deciles. In 2010 the richest, tenth decile of Stockholmers was the only one with a net capital income, which amounted to 38 per cent of their disposable income.

The immediate cause of rising Swedish inequality is class-structured capital investment and the turn of the liberalized Stockholm Stock Exchange, which for 1960–79 declined in average value, and then soared, outpacing the New York Stock Exchange by 10 per cent annually in the 1980s and 1990s (Roine and Waldenström 2012: 583). Capital income has become more important in Sweden than in continental Europe: a good 11 per cent of total household income in 2008 (Statistics

Sweden 2010: table 39), but only 7 per cent in Germany and 4 in France (OECD 2011a: Country Notes – Germany, France).

At the other end of the income hierarchy, the immediate causes are different. In the US, the legal minimum wage fell from about 45 per cent of the average wage to *circa* 30 per cent in 2004 (Mishel et al. 2009: 211). De-unionization was given two major governmental boosts in the 1980s: Reagan's dismissal of all striking traffic controllers, and Thatcher's defeat of the miners. At the same time, both politicians were lionizing Polish Solidarity, and revered in turn by Polish anti-Communists, for a brief while parading as trade unionists. Labour market insecurity – sold as 'flexibility' – became a paradigmatic policy, and unemployment benefits were cut, in duration as well as in amount.

These measures go along with an almost universal trend of increasing violations of basic labour rights from the mid-1980s to the early 2000s (Mosley 2011: 122f.). In Europe – Eastern as well as Western – labour rights have held up better than in other parts of the world. A major British workplace survey study found a mix of developments from the mid-1980s to the mid-2000s: greater use of workers' skills and reduced job insecurity in the early millennium boom, together with a collapse of collective bargaining, a decline in worker autonomy, and a net negative effect of 'high-involvement management', increasing anxiety. The Labour government's introduction of a National Minimum Wage and subsequent ratcheting it up seem to be the best explanation for a new pattern of wage growth for 1996–2003, when the lowest 10 per cent of wages increased more than the median (Brown et al. 2009: 175, 202f., 354f.). A similar, shortlived trend for the better for the lowest-paid occurred in the US in the 1990s with a temporary restoration of the minimum wage (Mishel et al. 2009: 156, 211).

Recent Latin American equalization has been the direct opposite of the situation in the US in the last few decades, positively supporting the poor and the people on the lower rungs of the labour market pyramid. Popular education has been rapidly extended, the minimum wage has been raised, social entitlements have been extended. Skill differentials in payment have gone down. Targeted social programmes have lifted many people out of extreme poverty, and increased schooling and child health (Lustig et al. 2012a, b). The overall decline of inequality has been modest, except perhaps in Venezuela, because little has been done at the top, against the entrenched affluence of the richest 10 per cent and of their dictat-ship over the state, which still has much less redistributive effect than the US government (see table 6 above).

Labour's share of value added produced has fallen in the world since about 1990, but, contrary to simple globalization models, most strongly outside the OECD core of capitalism, in North Africa and the Middle East, in sub-Saharan Africa and (intriguingly) in Latin America (OECD 2012: 71).

In brief, the top side of intra-national inequality is driven primarily by capital expansion and concentration, and that at the bottom by (politically alterable) policies to keep the poor down and softened up to accept anything.

These two pincers of current inequality both derive from recent transformations of world capitalism. At their core is a historical re-structuration. It began with a technological turn to de-industrialization, visible in the OECD labour statistics from about 1965, and accelerating after the first oil crisis of 1973–4. Soon, from the 1980s, there developed a dramatic financialization of developed capitalism, driven, at least in part, by deregulation of currency markets and stock exchange operations (the London 1986 Big Bang).

De-industrialization and an electronically possible expansion of private productive forces diminished the resources of labour, its concentration and its cohesion. While the moral responsibility for the recent defeats of labour may be pinned on employers and politicians bent on squeezing workers like lemons, the causal explanation of why they have been able to do so is another matter, referring to structural transformations. A crucial mechanism is likely to be a vicious spiral of growing resource inequality and what we identified above as political dictat-ship. De-industrialization and electronic management weaken the cohesiveness as well as the size of labour, financialization and the trans-nationalization of capital expand the power resources of capital, and the political policy process tilts in the favour of the latter, resulting in more pro-capital policies, which in turn makes the dictats of capital yet stronger and harsher.

Apart from its intrinsic structural change, of de-industrialization and financialization, world capitalism has also experienced an enormous extension, with the incorporation of most of the previous Communist economies into the world market. The world market entry of Chinese workers alone meant an increase of more than double the labour force of the OECD countries (OECD 2007: tables 1.2, 1.A.1.3). Global capital–labour relations cannot have been unaffected by this, tilting towards capital, even if, in recent years, as Marx would have predicted, rapid Chinese accumulation of capital has also led to stronger and more demanding labour there.

In terms of inequality mechanisms, financialization, pooled finance and electronically amplified 'star' performances have brought about an enormous distanciation of the top from the rest. At the bottom, political exclusion from (or lowering of) social protection and managerial re-hierarchization (with de-unionization) have pushed the most vulnerable further down the stairs.

The Contraflow of Gender

However, income distribution is not only bound up with capitalism, but also with existential relations – above all, of course, with those of the male–female halves of humankind. Here, income inequality is currently moving, slowly, in contraflow. Women's participation in paid labour has changed little on a world scale in the past decade, in spite of advances in Latin America. It remains about two-thirds of the male rate. In the Middle East and North Africa, it is still hardly more than a third of male labour market chances; in South Asia, about 40 per cent (ILO 2010: table A8).

But the pay gap is narrowing almost everywhere, with very substantial changes in Japan and Mexico – from a very wide start, though. Across occupations, women's earnings are now 85–90 per cent of men's in a number of countries, from Thailand and Russia to the UK, dipping to 81–2 per cent in Brazil and the USA. In 1973, American women's median wage earnings were only 63 per cent of men's, slightly worse than the current situation of South Korean women (two-thirds of male earnings) (UN 2010: 96ff.; USA: Mishel et al. 2009: 178).

In the UK, the gender gap for full-time employees declined from 17 to 12 per cent between 1998 and 2009 (Office of National Statistics 2010: 66).

8

Three Puzzles of
Contemporary Inequalities

Recent historical trajectories and current world patterns provide us with the three great puzzles. Why haven't the Northern European welfare states been able to deal better with vital inequality? Why has existential equalization been a post-World War II success story? Is there a connection between the simultaneous turns to international income equalization and to intra-national unequalization? So far, none of them has received much scholarly attention.

Why Have the Northern Welfare States Failed on Vital Inequality?

A series of studies has established that the socioeconomically and existentially relatively egalitarian Nordic welfare states have no distinguished record on class-based vital inequality (Kunst 1997; Mackenbach et al. 1997; Mackenbach et al. 2008), although they are not bad, an outcome very different from their decidedly respectable record on social security and equality. In terms of national infant and child mortality rates, the record of the Nordic countries is second only to Japan. With respect to premature adult mortality, before the age of 60, the picture is more uneven. Sweden again has the best record, together with Switzerland, and Norway is also doing very well, but Danish premature mortality is above the Western European average, for women as well as for men, and worse than that of the UK. Finnish women are roughly in the Western European middle, but Finnish men die prematurely almost as often as Americans, and have the steepest slope of social inequality in Europe (Rajaratnam et al. 2010: 1710–12).

European – and in particular Western European – premature adult mortality, and socially unequal risks for it, are mainly driven by cardiovascular diseases, and among them by ischemic heart disease, which is an inadequate blood supply to the heart (Mackenbach et al. 2008: table 2). The major immediate causes of heart and blood vessel diseases are known even to lay people like myself: smoking, animal fats, cholesterol, obesity, lack of exercise, etc. Their social configurations are less known, but we should not forget the findings of the great Whitehall study. Mortality from coronary heart disease followed the bureaucratic ladder step by step even after controlling for age, smoking, systolic blood pressure, plasma cholesterol concentration, height and blood sugar (Marmot 2004: 45). The lower your status in the hierarchy, the greater your risk of an early death.

As a non-physician, I am abstaining from any further speculation about causes of death. But the question of why the relatively egalitarian Nordic welfare states have had so little success in reducing vital inequality is more a socio-political than a medical question.

Vital inequality differs from the other two kinds of inequality in having a negative asymmetry of information at its heart. As far as existential and resource inequality go, it is usually the disadvantaged themselves who are the best informed. The nineteenth-century labour movement formulated it this way: the emancipation of the working class must be the work of the working class itself. True, there have been many social movements with demands referring to what we here call vital inequality, from bread riots which started the Russian February Revolution to the African food riots against IMF-imposed 'structural adjustment' in the 1980s. There have been struggles for decent housing, for access to health care, and against industrial and military destruction of the local environment. However, the fact remains – and now in particular, because of the recent advances of medical science – that the most vulnerable know least what food and medical treatment are best for their children, what diet and 'lifestyle' are best for their health.

This asymmetry of information runs even deeper. It is only quite recently that medical science has discovered the profound, even deadly, psychosomatic effects of social stress, of social hierarchies and of combinations of external demands and lack of control over one's work and/or life situation. This knowledge has hardly reached beyond specialists of social medicine as yet.

The limitations of lay knowledge are further compounded by constraints of choice. For many, the choice is not between a good healthy job and a bad risky job, but between a bad job and no job at all. And unemployment is even worse for your health (please remember ch. 1 above). Furthermore, some of the means to cope in the short run with a miserable life have dire longer-term consequences for your body: sweets, fats, nicotine, alcohol in doses for momentary oblivion, narcotic drugs. For many poor single mothers, it has been found, a cigarette is the one little luxury they allow themselves.

Immediate bodily harm and physically unsafe jobs, on the other hand, operate under a positive asymmetry of information. The people at risk know most about it. Job safety (*Arbeiterschutz*, or workers' protection) was a central concern of the early labour movement, and insurance against accidents at work, workmen's compensation, often the first social policy legislation. But it is difficult to build and sustain a social movement, and to create a winnable political agenda, about medical mechanisms operating over the long term that you do not quite fully understand. The current substitution of mercenary high-tech armed forces for the mass armies of the industrial age has also taken away one major historical reason for political elites to pay attention to the health of their population. More than a century ago, the disastrous British Boer War, and the experience that up to 40 per cent of the citizens who volunteered for the imperial army were found physically unfit for service, led the Tory Balfour government in 1904 to set up an Inter-Departmental Committee on Physical Deterioration (Frijters et al. 2009: 41).

It is easier when blame can be attached to a specific substance, be it asbestos, nicotine or alcohol. Dangerous substances without any intoxicating effects can be banned; dangerous stimulants can be contained by regulations and pricing. But prohibition does not work in the latter type of cases, which should be known from the days of Al Capone but apparently is not among the politicians making the decisions, as the current narcotics trade wars demonstrate. And even when elite opinion happens to be correct, as on smoking and fats, people in the popular classes have learnt so many times over generations that upper-class opinions had better not be swallowed whole.

The above is not incompatible with the plausible hypothesis that the Nordic social politicians have been facing bigger cultural challenges than their Mediterranean colleagues. The strong current association of heart diseases with low social status seems to be a rather recent phenomenon, first noticed in the United States in the 1950s, spreading to Northern Europe in the 1960s, and reaching Southern Europe only in the 1980s (Kunst 1997: 168ff.; Valkonen 1998: 287ff.). Animal fats, tobacco and a sedentary life were historically privileges of the more affluent. By historical irony, when this kind of consumption came within popular reach, as a manifestation of modest prosperity, medical science began telling the elites that it was unhealthy and dangerous. It was more of a problem in Northern (and Eastern) Europe than in the Mediterranean region because of different dietary cultures. Consumption of olive oil, vegetables and fish have kept both the incidence and the social differentials – or gradients, as they are called in social medicine – relatively low in Southern Europe. In Sweden, if you go down from higher to basic education, the number of deaths from cardiovascular diseases increases by 309 premature deaths annually per 100,000 population; in France, by 232; and on average, for three provinces in Spain, by 47.

Smoking and alcohol-caused deaths are less socially unequal in the three Scandinavian countries than in Southern Europe, which might be interpreted as a slightly successful public regulation, especially if seen against the background of Sweden's historical belonging to the Northeastern European vodka culture. The Finns, on the other hand, have the highest cardiovascular inequality in Western Europe, the second highest smoking inequality, and the third inequality in alcohol-related mortality. The East-Central European countries, from Slovenia to Estonia, are more lethally unequal than Western Europe, including Finland, in almost all respects. The only significant exception is death from cardiovascular disease in Slovenia, a Mediterranean country, with a class mortality differential of 405, almost the same as Switzerland and the UK (Mackenbach et al. 2008: table 2; mortality data from the 1990s in Western Europe, in East-Central from the late 1990s – early 2000s).

A Panglossian commentator of North Atlantic vital inequality might conclude that we are here seeing a transitory distanciation. Health knowledge has first spread to the upper classes, and, sooner or later, the populace will follow, and inequality will bend down. In other words, a kind of medical Kuznets curve. This hypothesis is not to be excluded a priori – it is obviously conceivable, and we may be confined to asking: 'How many will have to die before "sooner or later"?' But the recent jumps in vital inequality, from post-Communist Europe to the USA, via Finland, indicate that is unlikely. And the original Kuznets curve itself is out of date in contemporary capitalist economics of soaring income inequality in the most developed countries of the world.

Why Has Existential Egalitarianism become so Successful?

Existential egalitarianism is a great – if far from complete and not everywhere irreversible – success story of the past half-century or more. Enormous egalitarian advances have been made in race, settler–indigenous, gender and sexual relations. Disabled people have been able to emerge out of shunted-off closets, provided with rights and supports. How did this come about? Why has existential egalitarianism suddenly become so uniquely successful?

In one sense, it all started in 1945. True, there was a moment of existential equalization in the anti-monarchical, anti-aristocratic Atlantic revolutions of the late eighteenth to early nineteenth centuries, which so preoccupied Alexis de Tocqueville, the Americo-phile French liberal aristocrat. But in still-hegemonic Europe, the *anciens régimes* persisted, as Arno Mayer (1981) has reminded us, from the Court of St James to Tsarskoe Selo. The cosmopolitanism of the Enlightenment was succeeded by an imperialist racism of continuously mounting virulence, culminating in the World War II policies of the powers of the Anti-Comintern Pact. If they had won the war, our success story would have been called off, at least for a century.

The total defeat of Nazi Germany, militaristic Japan and Fascist Italy did set the décor of a new historical stage. The finest piece was the UN Declaration of Human Rights, adopted in December 1948, the product of a handful of imaginative lawyers, guided by the skilled diplomacy of Eleanor Roosevelt (Glendon 2001). But at the time it was no more than an angelic vision of another world, where 'race colour, sex, language, religion, political or other opinion, national or social origin, property, birth or other status' had no bearing on rights (Article 2.1). Even off the centre of hardcore high politics, its article on adult freedom to marriage, 'without any limitation due to race, nationality or religion', and 'equal rights . . . during marriage' (Article 16.1) was then no more than an enlightened wish. In 1948, only the Scandinavian countries lived up to the Article. Arranged marriages were prevalent all over Asia and Africa, frequent in the Balkans, and in Andean America. A large number of US states prohibited inter-racial marriage; Greece and Muslim countries prohibited inter-religious marriages. The Soviet Union, which was the only country outside Scandinavia proclaiming equal rights within marriage, was putting increasing restrictions on inter-national marriage. Most countries, including Europe south of Scandinavia, had legislated husband domination within marriage (see further Therborn 2004).

The beautiful décor had few egalitarian actors on stage. In many ways, the total surrender of Nazi Germany was not the real beginning. And, tellingly enough, the lawyer behind the anti-Jewish Nuremberg Laws, Hans Globke, survived into the new era, as a backstage fixer for West German Chancellor Adenauer.

Imperial racism and racist imperialism re-ignited immediately, as if Auschwitz was another planet. The French were particularly untroubled by any conceptions of human rights. Not only did they everywhere re-conquer their colonies, they also immediately started massacring any native protest, Algerian demonstrators in Sétif and mutinous Senegalese soldiers, with contractual payments unpaid, already before the end of 1945 (Therborn and Bekker 2012: 198). The British had understood they were incapable of holding on to India, but they put up vicious colonial wars in Malacca and in Kenya, with Boer War-type concentration camps in the former, and sadistic torture in the latter case, just recently belatedly recognized by British courts. The Dutch tried to re-conquer Indonesia, and the Belgians returned to Kongo.

In the US after the war, most institutionalized racism remained intact, officially in the South, and de facto in the North, although the army was officially de-segregated in 1948. Theatres, cinemas, hotels and restaurants remained racially segregated, in Washington until the early 1950s. In the Soviet Union, the last years of Stalin saw a sudden outburst of official anti-Semitism, hitting even Olga Molotova, the wife of Stalin's ever loyal foreign minister.

But the best exhibit for the case of 1945 as a non-starter is what happened in South Africa. There, the postwar meant the triumph of the most rabid racism in imperial history. The National Party, which included pro-Nazi currents from wartime, won the White elections from 1948 on, and established apartheid, separating the White master race from the servant races in all walks of life, from politics and business to park benches and beaches. Apartheid was not genocidal. The South African rulers depended upon Black subjugated labour. But short of genocide, it was the most elaborate racist doctrine ever put into practice. Virulent racism in South Africa since the late 1940s did not meet any significant international opprobrium until the 1960s – after the 1960 massacre at Sharpeville – and faced biting isolation and sanctions only from the late 1970s.

Existential equalization depends primarily on the strength and the struggles of the disadvantaged themselves. But a historian of social change had better pay attention to triggering or tipping events, as well as to the accumulation of social force. The US Supreme Court decision in 1954, in *Brown* vs *Board of Education*, that racial school segregation was unconstitutional, opened a watershed in American race relations – not in itself, but as a social and political trigger. Racist resistance was ferocious, violent and tenacious, for more than a decade, by local police and state governments as well as by lynch mobs and murder squads. But in the context of Cold War competition, the Federal government saw that it had to defend the US Constitution and US international reputation. In 1957, Federal troops were sent to Little Rock, Arkansas, to protect the new constitutional right of desegregated schooling. That did not decide the issue, though, and violence went on. The full weight of the Federal government, police and Congress was not deployed until the mid-1960s. During this protracted struggle, a broad Civil Rights movement emerged, fighting against racial humiliations on public transport as well as against the racist denial of African Americans' right to vote. It finally won in the late 1960s, almost two centuries after the Declaration of Independence proclaimed it 'self-evident' that 'all men are born equal'.

To women, 1945 meant the right to vote in Latin Europe, and gradually Latin America; a wonderful

Japanese Constitution and Family Law; and a historic advance of social and family rights in Eastern Europe. The Chinese Communist Revolution sparked off a dramatic change of family and gender norms, which, against strong patriarchal peasant resistance, took a generation to be realized (Therborn 2004: 92ff.).

Without social strength, without sustained social struggle, there can be no existential equalization. So, whence sprang the sources of strength, and what did the paths of successful struggle look like?

The international context was favourable, and increasingly so. The Communists had their revolutionary programme from the classics of Marxism, and the American occupation of Japan aimed at cutting off the social roots of Japanese militarism, something which by a lucky accident came to include a Feminist edge. By war and through hard bargaining, decolonization was advancing, filling up the United Nations, and shrinking the global space for racism. While neither particularly egalitarian nor beacons of human rights, the growing and increasingly influential Communist bloc had a positive impact on existential equality in the world. It was anti-racist, and it was not patriarchal. In the competition for global hegemony, domestic racism and support for racist regimes like South Africa were mounting liabilities. Egalitarian gender and family relations were not yet a hegemonic asset. However, they could, and were, used in shrewd diplomatic manoeuvres with important egalitarian outcomes. Most significant was the tremendously successful and influential UN Conference on Women in 1975 in Mexico. It originated in an initiative by the Women's International Democratic Federation, a Communist organization associated with the UN (see further Therborn 2004: 76). The UN Convention on the Rights of the Child had a similar background: an initiative of the Polish Politburo, wanting to push the emerging international human rights concerns in a different

direction, and drawing upon an old Polish pre-war tradition of progressive paediatrics (Therborn 1996: 42).

Domestic developments were decisive, though.
Unprecedented postwar industrial and service economy
growth drained large parts of the Southern American
and later South African countryside of the old master–
slave relations. Industrial and urban Black employment
and basic education expanded. In South Africa, increasing scarcity of White industrial workers pushed the
colour bar upwards from the late 1960s (Seekings and
Nattrass 2006: 20).

Secondary and higher education also expanded, providing downtrodden groups with articulate, well-
informed spokespersons and cadres. The core of the US
Civil Rights movement were college students, a fearless
vanguard in the Freedom Summer of 1964. The Feminist movement rose as a mass movement among university students and young academics. Gay Liberation
Fronts and organized Lesbianism emerged too from the
student movements and milieux of 1968.

The new outspokenness of indigenous peoples can
also in several cases be traced to the rise of modern
educated advocates in their midst. But they have hardly
been much drawn into the modern economy, before
recent mining forays from India to Peru. What has
changed their situation is their becoming connected to
the rest of the world, globally as well as nationally,
through electronic communication, and through international organizations, sometimes through the UN or
the World Social Fora.

Strength and struggle, in a favourable global context,
have sustained advances towards existential equality in
the world. The contrast with conditions of income inequality in the most recent decades is stark. Weakening
from de-industrialization, outsourcing, union busting,
neoliberal politics, crucial defeats in industrial struggles,
and outwitted by the neoliberal shock commanders

after the implosion of Communism, even the once powerful Polish *Solidarnosc* turned into a ghost. An international context of global financialization and aggressive
neoliberalism drove income equality backwards.

However, matters get a bit more complicated, and
intriguing, when we consider the divergent politics and
temporalities of resource and existential inequality.
Existential equalization is continuing in most parts of
the world, not least including neoliberal NATOland.
The enormous increase in US economic inequality led
up to the election of the country's first ever Black president, and income gaps of race and gender have narrowed under the soaring sun of the 1 per cent. In 2010
the median income of African-American households
was 38 per cent lower than the White median, enough
for all egalitarians to cry foul, but in 1980 the race differential was 42 per cent. Women have done much
better, cutting the full-time earnings differential from 40
per cent in 1980 to 23 per cent in 2010 (Noah 2012:
44–5). In the heartlands of advanced capitalism, the
period of 1945–80 was a period of equalization. In spite
of the total defeat of Nazi racism in 1945, racial equalization only got going in the 1960s, when the cautious
US steps of the 1950s were no longer balanced by
continuously more aggressive apartheid, and when
Africa began to be decolonized. Resource equalization
started directly after the War – following upon wartime
equalizations.

In other words, what has, so far, made existential
equalization sustainable, and income equalization not?
A crucial difference between the two inequalities is that
one is usually a zero-sum game; the other is not necessarily so. Resource inequality means unequal command
of resources, with which you can buy whatever you
want, from sex objects to secluded ocean-front man-
sions, or political influence. As a privileged beneficiary
of existential inequality you can bask in the deference

of your subordinates and be satisfied that the unworthy are kept in their place. With income equalization, you would lose your competitive edge over others, your capacity to throw Berlusconi-style 'bunga-bunga' parties, to keep your own jet or your own Caribbean island. Existential equalization, by contrast, does not in itself change your advantageous life chances – unless you are a sadist. Everybody gets a chance to develop her life-dreams, and the fact that a Black Lesbian single mother, or an Inuit seal hunter, gets a chance does not affect life within the Washington Beltway or in the Home Counties of the UK. Moreover, existential income discrimination does not make much sense to financial capital. No banker risks his bonus if the average income of Blacks or of women should go up.

There is one exception to this condition of existential inequality. That is where it is based on what Charles Tilly (1998) named a pairing of categories – that is, when the superiority of one category is derived from the inferiority of the other. That was the case of race relations in the American and the African South, where the affluence and the good life of the Whites depended on the cheap labour and the misery of the Blacks. Thence the vicious resistance of the former. It was undone by changed relations of resources, which tipped the struggles in a new direction. In current industrial and post-industrial economies, that racially exploitative pairing is no longer quite relevant, although the so-called 'creative classes' of NATOland are increasingly dependent on immigrant servants, like their likes in the Gulf and in Hong Kong and Singapore. However, these 'creators' of the universe do not derive their wealth from the labour of their servants.

To what extent male superiority in the past was based on paired exploitation of women is something that I shall leave unexplored in this context. However, current male enrichment is hardly affected by women's rights.

Male career paths may become more competitive, which has produced some male resistance, but there is also, and increasingly, the case that a man will benefit, economically and socially, from having an economically successful wife.

Having to accept that indigenous peoples have their own history and culture, or that homosexuals have the same right to sexuality as heteros, may be culturally irritating to some – who therefore resist. But for many people, and especially the urbane, well-heeled elites of the neoliberal dispensation, it is no big deal – and to some a claim to enlightenment.

Existential inequality has been a pest of modern as well as of ancient history. The dismantling of it in recent years is a major human advance. It has been able to move forward because – and to the extent that – it has been decoupled from resource inequality. Standing alone, with rotting economic props of racism, sexism, etc., against resourceful and angry humiliated people, existential inequality has had difficulty resisting, while powerful elites have found the issue a gift of costless egalitarianism. It has also benefited from silence on deeper, more controversial issues, such as the correlation between hierarchy and death.

Is There a Connection between Recent Inter-national Convergence and Intra-national Unequalization?

The major economic intra-national equalization in modern history ended around 1980, in the rich OECD area of the North Atlantic, Japan and Oceania. At about the same time – exact dating dependent on different kinds of estimates – inter-national, global inequality started to decline, after a continuous rise of almost two centuries. Is there a connection, and if so, what is it?

Instead of at the easily available scapegoat 'globaliza-tion', available evidence points in the opposite direction, towards coincidental – at most, indirectly related – developments.

Rising economic inequality in the world, which started to ascend in the early nineteenth century, flat-tened out after World War II, measured in terms of population-weighted per capita national income. A polarization between the rich and the poorest countries is still going on until this day, though. The main global equalizers have been China and India, as poor countries with fast growth. The end of overall global unequaliza-tion was about 1950, the time of Indian independence and of the Chinese Revolution. At that nadir, Chinese GDP per capita was the same as in year 1 Christian Era (!), and the Indian GDP somewhere between the per capita product of 1873 and of 1913 (Maddison 2007: table A7). Urban Indian real wages could be lower than in Agra in 1595 (Allen 2005: 121). Annual economic growth per capita had been negative in India as well as in China for the period of 1913–50, and more or less stagnant or negative before that. Then the big Asian economies started to grow, by 2.8 per cent a year in China and 1.4 in India. The change after the Revolution /Independence (1950–73), with a qualitative turn from economic decline to growth, is numerically even some-what larger than the differences in per capita GDP com-pared to the previous period between pre-liberal 1973–90 and neoliberal 1990–2003 for both China and India (Maddison 2007: 171, 382–3). The often-touted growth effect of Indian liberalization in 1990–1 spawned an extra 1.3 per cent annual per capita growth over the 1973–90 period.

National self-determination made a historical differ-ence in both cases. This clearly had nothing to do with domestic inequality in the rich world, which at the time was on its way down. Nor is there any conceivable link between China's capitalist turn around 1980 and North Atlantic distribution. It was around 1980 that, in retrospect, we can discern a slight bend downwards of the population-weighted inter-national income inequality curve, which only started rolling about 1990 (Milanovic 2012: figure 2). There is no plausible common cause of recent global equalization and simultaneous intra-national unequalization of income. Nor is there any visible causal arrow running from Euro-American domestic inequality to a less unequal world.

But is the link perhaps the other way around, from the rise of China and other poor countries to rich world inequality? There are some suspects, already pointed at in the public debate: outsourcing of production, outward foreign investment from NATOland, low-waged competitive trade from China and lots of other new export manufacturers. While the econometric discussion of the issue is far from concluded, the current tendency of expert opinion is to regard the above as minor culprits.

A recent report by the economic organization of the world's richest countries, the OECD, finds no significant effect of general trade globalization, though one of imports from low-income countries and only a modest effect of outward foreign investment on the widening dispersion of earnings – and the latter balanced by the other side of financial opening, equalization from foreign investment into OECD countries. Domestic inequality in the rich world has been driven, the OECD team of economists argue econometrically, primarily by lower unionization, lower employment protection (i.e., increasing precariousness of temporary work), lower unemployment compensation, less redistributive taxation and product markets deregulation (OECD 2011a: ch. 2, esp. tables 2.1, 2.2 and 2.3).

In other words, successful export competition from China and other poor countries has affected

rich-country internal inequality, but hardly in any decisive direct way. Much more important has been the
weakening of labour's rights and collective opportunities. True, part of this may be seen as adaptation to
external competitive pressure. But the most spectacular
aspect of rich-country intra-national inequality, the ballooning of the 1 per cent, cannot be ascribed to the
Chinese and the other 'emerging' economies. Its winner-
takes-all dynamics is not unrelated to 'globalization',
but it derives from the globalized reach and power of
the Euro-American economic elites, as we noticed above.
And the power of the rulers of advanced capitalism is
still differentially embedded in national state structures
and societal configurations. Germany and Japan, two of
the world's export giants, have had very modest inequality increases, and the Japanese system of public
redistribution, low to begin with, has been substantially
ratcheted up in the last decades. France, another country
difficult to dismiss, has had a very modest recent increase
in inequality, which still leaves the richest 10 per cent
with a smaller share of national income than in 1985
(OECD 2011a: Country Notes – France, Germany,
Japan).

We may find an interrelated class–state background
to inter-national equalization and intra-national unequalization. A more connected world, of trade, finance
and communications, has created new possibilities, for
elites of self-determined developmental states as well as
for the most powerful and the most privileged of the
rich countries, possibilities to a not insignificant extent
dependent on institutional structures and social constellations. The world has been prised open to rapacious
forces in the South as well as in the North, boosting
Southern national income, from which crumbs have
fallen also to the poor, and to the pathetic 'middle class'
living on more than $2 a day (cf. Ravaillon 2010).
However, national politics still matters, as is indicated

by the (modest) decline of inequality in Latin American countries, in spite of increasing commodities rents, from soybeans to oil and all kinds of mining.

A class dynamic of intra-national polarization is operating both North and South, which may connect social movements across the equator. A new pathway for such connections is now running through consumer-*cum*-trade-union concerns in the North with exploitative, outsourced suppliers from the South, bringing pressure most directly on the big Northern retailers, like the biggest and the most vicious, Walmart, and designer brands like Apple or Nike.

V

Possible Futures

Current inequalities are no fatality. They can be changed, increased as well as reduced. They have been in the past. What perspectives of change are there? What are the key issues? What is the line-up of social forces? Where are the likely decisive battlefields?

9

Overcoming Inequality – Yesterday and Tomorrow

Inequalities are social constructions, and as such amenable to deconstruction. As we have seen already, their history is not linear, either upwards or downwards. (In)Equality has always been located in historical situations.

Moments of Equality

In modern history there have been epochal moments of equality of four major kinds. None of them had any focus on vital inequality, although in some cases there was a substantial expansion of public health care.

One such moment was in the great revolutions. The French Revolution focused on existential equality among male citizens – as did American Independence, though less dramatically – but, in contrast to the latter, the former also produced substantial equalization of resources, largely by land reform but also through a hike in urban real wages (Morrisson 2000: 235ff.). The Russian, the Chinese, and more local Communist

revolutions brought about drastic resource equalizations, often in brutal ways, of housing space as well as
of land and income.[15] Communist revolutionary equalization also extended to gender relations, attacking
entrenched patriarchy head-on (Therborn 2004: 83ff.,
93ff.). The Chinese and the Cuban Revolutions, in particular, spread health care to the countryside, undone in
post-Maoist China in the 1990s but proudly maintained
by the Cubans even in that dire decade. In Eastern
Europe, the life expectancy gap with Western Europe
narrowed from ten years in 1930 to two years in 1965,
after which it began to widen again (for detailed refer-
ences, see Therborn 1995: table 8.3).

While falling far short of egalitarian utopias, the
revolutions left legacies of equalization. The advances
of the French Revolution largely survived the royal
counter-revolution imposed by Britain and Tsarist
Russia. On the eve of the capitalist turn in Russia and
China, income inequality was among the lowest in the
world, although somewhat behind the geopolitically
lucky reformisms of Scandinavia, with a Russian Gini
coefficient of 0.26 in 1989 and a Chinese one of 0.32
in 1978 (Cornia et al. 2004: 30, 33).

Second, more widespread and more violent, were the
two industrial World Wars, greatly affecting economic
distribution in Europe, North America and Japan. Both
hit the *rentier* class hard, as we noticed above. Their
mobilization of the total population for national industrial war came to facilitate existential equalization

[15] Whether the agrarianist, anti-urban, anti-industrial ethno-
'purifying' take-over of power by the Khmer Rouge qualifies
as a Communist revolution or not is open to debate – it was
only recognized as such by Maoists. In any case, it was, of
course, a mass-murderous regime without any positive social
relevance, for a while given UN legitimacy, as an anti-
Vietnamese pawn, by the US and its UN allies.

– both wars with respect to women's political rights; the second, through the smashing defeat of Germany and Japan, at least discrediting, if not abolishing, blatant racism.

Third, the 1930s Depression spawned game-changing egalitarian regimes of varying depth and longevity in several countries: the New Deal in the USA, Social Democracy in Scandinavia, and the Popular Front in France. The crisis blow to the City of London also meant a scaling-down of top UK incomes (Atkinson et al. 2010: 711ff.). But the Great Depression had a contradictory impact. It heightened racism in several countries, in Germany and its allies above all. Eugenics spread in Scandinavia, and one of the indispensable pillars of the New Deal coalition was the Southern Democrats, whose vicious racism had to be accommodated. Labour market gender discrimination also rose, particularly in Europe south of Scandinavia and west of the USSR.

Violent revolutions, large-scale industrial wars, profound economic crisis – strong storms have been necessary to tame the ferocious anti-egalitarianism of late-feudal, patriarchal and modern capitalist societies. However, there has also been a fourth kind of egalitarian moment. Under certain circumstances, far-reaching peaceful social reform has been possible. This is obviously the experience most relevant to the current world.

Here we have two examples – one major, but historical and currently being undermined, in vital as well as in income respects. That was virtually the whole developed capitalist world from the aftermath of World War II until about 1980, with egalitarian advances of existential rights and respect and a general equalization of health and life expectancy, as well as major national equalizations of resources of income and education. The process accelerated in the 1960s and early 1970s, with rapid expansion of social services and transfer payments, and a crack in male domination and advantage. The '1968' movements were part of this larger egalitarian period – without recognizing it as such – as well as a motor of its acceleration.

This was also a global moment of equality, above all existentially, with decolonization, the defeat of institutionalized racism and the breakthrough of women's rights in the 1970s, but also in vital respects through the global diffusion of vaccination, public hygiene and preventive medicine. Economically, China and independent South Asia started to grow, and Northeast Asian capitalism embarked on a new, relatively egalitarian path of national development.

The other example is still minor in achievement, and its long-term political sustainability is an open question. But it has the advantage of being pursued in current real time. Since 2002, with two minor exceptions – Costa Rica and the Dominican Republic – Latin America has been bucking the global trend of increasing domestic income inequality. From Andean heights of inequality, Latin America is currently the only world region where economic inequality is climbing down (CEPAL 2012: 21). At the same time, existential equalization is moving ahead, with respect to Indian populations – above all in now officially 'plurinational' Bolivia and the other Andean countries – and to 'Afro-descendants', especially in Brazil.

What have been the politico-economic contexts of these two periods of peaceful substantial equalization? They are very different in their historical location, but they have two striking features in common. First, in both region-periods, rapid economic growth was an important macroeconomic context, much easing the frictions of social investment and reproduction. Also significant, for its social sustainability, is the character of the boom, its generality, producing more or less full employment in developed capitalism and increasing formal-sector employment in Latin America.

Second, and at least as important, in both cases, right-wing liberalism was utterly discredited and kept out of the political centre, associated with the inter-war Depression and its mass unemployment or, in Latin America, with the military dictatorships and the economic disasters of the 1980s–1990s. Right-wing authoritarian anti-liberalism had virtually disappeared, buried in the *Führerbunker* of Berlin or under the rubble of Hiroshima and Nagasaki in the first case, and discarded with the nightmares of the military juntas in Latin America. In short, the two most militant anti-egalitarian forces in modern history were politically incapacitated – though not fatally, as it would turn out in the liberal case.

Are the above necessary preconditions of a successful surge in equality? Social theory finds it difficult to say, but American-*cum*-Scandinavian experience of the Depression clearly suggests that a boom is not necessary. Ironically, it seems that it was the socially concerned welfare state which in 2008–9 rescued neoliberal finance capitalism from massive and utter discredit. The public bailouts stabilized the financial markets, and unemployment and other public benefits prevented the victims of the crisis from falling into the poverty and hunger of the 1930s, even in the US. The 2008 crisis protests, on the whole, therefore lacked the wrath and the despair of the 1930s, except perhaps in helpless Greece in its euro cage.

The political condition of a serious debilitation of the two foremost modern enemies of equality, economic liberalism and right-wing authoritarianism, looks much more plausible. And here, outside current Latin America, we are facing what Colin Crouch (2011) has called 'The Strange Non-Death of Neoliberalism'.

Politically, the civilian moments of equality have both been driven by broad, heterogeneous constellations, with motives ranging from pragmatic power calculations, among conservative North Atlantic leaders such as Adenauer in Germany, Yoshida in Japan, and Eisenhower and Nixon in the USA, to egalitarian political and social forces, from American Democrats to European Social and Christian Democracy, and social movements of labour, women's and civil rights. Particularly in the first period, conservatives and egalitarians had a common ground in a concern with national social cohesion, a value always despised by militant liberalism. It should not be forgotten that this was the time of the global Cold War and its systemic competition, and, from recent traumatic experience, a rejection in principle of any fundamental (existential) human inequality. Heteroclite coalitions and parallel movements have sustained the egalitarian thrusts of the Latin American presidencies of Lula, Chavez, Correa, Morales, Kirchner and others, but here this is more a manifestation of the heterogeneity of the Latin left-of-centre than of cross-spectrum de facto national alignments.

The economic and the political contexts of the egalitarian moments were auspicious, but they were not the deciding factors. People were, in social struggles. In the 1950s, it could be argued – and was argued – that now there was prosperity, social policies and redistribution are no longer needed. But from the left came the argument, now, for the first time, that we could afford to create a society of social security for everybody. In Sweden, for example, as I personally remember well, the second argument was the winning majority's argument, settling the issue in a series of dramatic elections over occupational pensions in the late 1950s – early 1960s. In the UK, Tory-propagated consumerism carried election days in 1955 and 1959, but not in a decisive way it was to appear in the 1960s. Not even in the USA was individual consumerism enough to stop egalitarian questions from being both raised and heard in the 1960s. Little wonder, then, that it could not prevent the rise of the welfare state on the European continent.

Latin American egalitarians are being confronted with the critical question: will egalitarianism be able to sustain (middle-class) economic development? Hitherto, high global oil prices have made it possible to sustain the most radical variant, in Venezuela, and also to fill the Treasuries of Bolivia and Ecuador, while the Lula–Dilma governments of Brazil have so far been able to combine extremely cost-effective redistributive measures with, by and large, Brazilian capitalism as usual.

How long the current egalitarian Latin American governments will be able to answer their critical question positively, or whether, in some cases, they will deliberately risk a social confrontation with the middle (and upper) classes (already happening in Venezuela and Bolivia), I have to leave unsaid. At least in the heavyweight case of Brazil, the economic prospects for egalitarian policies of social approximation, inclusion, de-hierarchization and redistribution look pretty good, with huge windfall rents soon to flow from deep-sea gas.

Forces of Equality

The deconstruction of inequalities will ultimately depend on the strength and the skills of the forces of equality. Who are they? From my historical studies of the rise of modern democracy and of the right to vote, I have learnt that, for an understanding of conflictual social change, it is not enough to look at the forces of demand and those of resistance. There are also forces of supply of change, i.e., forces of existing establishments who, for some reason, are willing to offer it from above. But let us begin by looking at forces of demand for equality, in the recent past, and possibly in the future.

Forces of demand

In the twentieth century, the major force of equality was the working-class and the labour movement, although, as we saw above, they always had to operate in a complex political environment, and their amount of success depended at least as much on their skills in manoeuvring this environment as on their numbers. They were the backbone of the struggles for democracy and the right to vote (Therborn 1977), for social rights and economic redistribution (Korpi 1983). The relatively egalitarian decades of core capitalism were the zenith of organized labour, in rates of unionization and in electoral votes (Therborn 1984). The most significant metropolitan support that the anti-colonial movements received came from sections of the labour movement, as did the most weighty – though often not very heavy – male support that the women's movement got – if it came at all with any weight (Therborn 2004: ch. 2).

Now the industrial working class is in decline in the centres of capitalism and the labour movement is in retreat almost everywhere, except in China, where it is growing but in very fragmented forms. It is providing a significant social compass in the ongoing Latin American process, particularly in Argentina, Bolivia and Brazil, but even there it is not the carrying force it once was for the Western European, and especially the Nordic, welfare states.

Egalitarian futures are even more likely to depend on wide and socioeconomically more heterogeneous social coalitions, within which industrial labour will remain an indispensable but not necessarily leading component. In what we used to call the Third World, there are the urban poor, of street vendors, casual or otherwise precarious labourers, middle-class employees, and peasants, with little or no land. In the rich centres of capitalism, the mobilization of the new servant class in the 'service sector', the inclusion of the immigrant subproletariat, and a rallying of a substantial part of the professional middle class appear to be crucial.

Categorical identity movements – of women, ethnic groups, lately homosexuals – have also been very important egalitarian forces, decisive with respect to their categorical demands, but very important also to general conceptions of economic as well as existential equality. The strength of these movements fluctuates conjuncturally, but it faces no structural decline. In contemporary Latin America, ethnic and racial movements and currents have become very important, explicitly and formally in Bolivia, informally in Venezuela. In multiethnic societies, such as in Africa and South and Southeast Asia, ethno-cultural movements may easily turn into exclusivist forces of difference and separation rather than of social equality. But there is a certainly a need, and hopefully a future, for civil rights movements in these regions, especially in South and Southeast Asia. The discrimination against, and poverty of, the Rohingya people, statelessly shuffled between Myanmar and Bangladesh, are horrendous, even by European standards (towards the Eastern European Roma).

The women's movements of Africa and Asia have tremendous mountains of inegalitarian hurdles and hindrances in front of them. Recent advances in female education make it a good bet that women's movements, especially in India and North Africa, will play an increasing role, demanding egalitarian change. In the rich world, the future of women's movements is difficult to predict. It should be noted, though, that the post-1968 turn of women to the left, reversing previous majority leanings to the (religious) right, has so far survived the opening both of corporate power and of CIA assassination squads to women. Not only gender equality, but social equality more generally, tends to have more female than male support.

There is also a current in the rich countries which we may call solidaristic individualism. Today it is not as influential as it once was because of new political constellations, in which wars are waged with mercenaries and unmanned drones, and racism has been made respectable by Zionist lobbies and by various currents recycling the 'Yellow Peril' of a century ago into an Islamic one. But it is reproduced into new generations, even in Israel, with all the courage and stamina that takes. This is the current behind the Northern consumer movements against labour exploitation in the South, and behind most of the worldwide environmentalist movements, and in particular the awareness of environmental inequality and injustice. Climate change affects the whole planet, but whose houses will be flooded? In other areas there will be droughts, and water has already become scarce, e.g. in West Asia and in Northern China – who will be supplied with water and who not? Who will have to live in the most polluted urban neighbourhoods?

Solidaristic individualism – 'I want to choose my own lifestyle, but I am concerned about the possibilities of others to make their choice' – is a vital force of equality. It provided the vibrant, albeit unsustainable, dynamic of the Occupy movements (see, further, Castells 2012; Mason 2012).

The new internet-based media may not have changed the parameters of politics as much as some of their boosters claim, as was manifested in the outcomes of the Arab Spring of 2011 and by the petering out of the Occupy movement, but they have certainly altered the preconditions of mass movements. At the moment of writing, there is no major campaign movement for equality in sight, but the response to calls for action from online activist groups such as Adbuster and the Avaaz campaigns make it more likely than not that, in the next few years, we will have a global campaign movement for Equality.

Forces of supply

Equality derives basically from demand. But as social equality is a social force of cohesion, of combat as well as of development, it has its forces of supply, driven first of all by fear. There is the fear of the unequals, of their anger and their possible protests and rebellion. Secondly, there is the fear of the external enemy, the fear of not being up to the lethal capacity of the latter. Thirdly, there is the fear of backwardness, and projects of inclusive national development. While fear is a basic source of equalization measures by the powerful and privileged, it is not the only one. Ruling elites and/or their staff are not always fully absorbed by their own privileges and greed. They are not necessarily incapable of comprehensive visions and far-sighted strategic calculations – occasionally even of empathy with their subjects.

In modern times, competition with Communism spurred capitalist and imperial elites to major measures of equalization. For instance, the US-supervised land reforms in South Korea and Taiwan, or the German Christian Democratic innovation in 1957 of the *dynamisierte Rente*, whereby pensions were linked to the (rising) development of real wages, meant as a social concession for securing German rearmament. The forceful intervention against Southern American racism by President Eisenhower, who never had any personal sympathy for African-American civil rights (Frank 2013), by sending federal paratroops to protect Black children against racist mobs in Little Rock, is impossible to imagine outside the Cold War context.

The consideration of Communist influence is now gone, and the new principal enemy for the US and its NATO hangers-on, radical political Islam, does not call for any mitigations of capitalist inequality – at most, some respect for conservative Muslim clerics and royal families.

Today's China is more unequal than the USA, not to speak of Europe, thus not very likely to entice egalitarian emulation. External development through national cohesion, the post-1945 Northeast Asian model, has not become an international lodestar, in spite of its historical success. Southeast Asia, for instance, seems to be more interested in offering itself up to foreign investors. The Arab oil emirates have been run with a certain sense of *noblesse oblige*, sadly lacking among most African Big Men, but their dependence on a harsh exploitation of imported labour makes their social states as social as slaveholding Ancient Athens was democratic.

Forces of egalitarian supply have become short in supply. Existential gender and sexual equality may get a boost from above, as we have seen recently in a few countries, from Argentina to France and Nepal. But few other probable national candidates are in sight. No general egalitarian impetus from any political establishment is to be expected in the foreseeable future. Equalization will have to fight its way up from below.

But there does remain one force of egalitarian supply, which seems to be growing rather than declining. There has developed a not insignificant professional humanist civility in the world. You find it in the UN institutions – above all, in the Development Programme (UNDP) which regularly measures the development of human inequality as well as human development; the ILO which is concerned with decent and indecent jobs, with employment precariousness and vulnerability; the WHO, preoccupied with the social determinants of health; the FAO with food (in)security; the UN Habitat with slums and urban inequality, etc.; and so on. The regional UN economic commissions are sometimes significant institutions of social concern, the Latin American CEPAL in particular. The World Bank is no longer a monolithic bastion of neoliberalism (if it ever was), and contains a number of the best researchers into world inequality. The economic organization of the rich world, the OECD, is increasingly widening its perspective, socially and spatially. The EU Commission has never paid much attention to (in)equality, but gender, and more recently, sexual attitudes and relations, have come increasingly to the fore in the EU, including in the parliamentary hearings of candidate commissioners.

The above bodies, with the exceptions of the least committed EU and World Bank, have no direct power. They are global or regional suppliers of knowledge – but also, hitherto, of social concerns.

10

The Decisive Battlefields of Future (In)Equality

Instead of counting the formidable forces of anti-egalitarian resistance, which will be re-shaped in the social struggles – as will the forces of equality – we shall here try to identify the decisive fields of battle. I think there are three. One concerns our comprehension of inequality. The second is a set of key social institutions, which have to be confronted and transformed for any major equalization to be possible. In the era of revolutions, there were attempts at abolishing them – with no or little success, as it turned out. In the current century of downsized expectations, we have to look for ways of reforming or regulating them.

The third crucial battlefield will be for the social allegiance which will decide, at least for the foreseeable future, the socio-political tipping-point between equality and inequality. The outcome of that political battle is likely to depend significantly – if far from exclusively – on how the forces of equality have been able to manage the first two.

The Image of Inequality

The easiest and most widespread egalitarianism is resentment of the rich. In today's remote-controlled and secluded world, it is also the most impotent. I suspect that most of the people whom former New Labour Cabinet Minister Peter Mandelson (with fond irony) called the 'filthy rich' deserve most of the resentment they occasionally receive – in between sycophantic admiration. But this little book has been written, largely, to argue that the wealth of Carlos Slim and the other billionaires is not the vilest villainy of the world. Inequality runs much deeper into human lives, causing millions of unnecessary, premature deaths, stunting lives across generations, producing humiliations, unfreedom, insecurity and anxiety for continent-sized populations across the globe. Its lethal effects, as we have seen above, seep even into well-heeled bureaucratic hierarchies of the rich world.

Bio-medicine has become a central knowledge frontier for humankind. What we have here been calling vital and existential inequalities, the interwoven inequalities of bodies and persons, have to become the focus of egalitarian debate and action. Although they each have a dynamic and an actual social trajectory of their own, the three kinds of inequality – vital, existential and resource – are all interacting and interdependent. The current drives of income inequality in the world have devastating social and political, as well as medical and psychological, effects, as I have also tried to demonstrate above.

The egalitarian focus has to be on all the multidimensional violations of, and man-made hindrances for, the capabilities of all humans to develop and to flourish. In the rich world, this means that the poster image of inequality should not be a *Forbes* billionaire, but a

London boy in Tottenham Green who, if not unusually unlucky, has seventeen years fewer to live than a fellow Londoner in Chelsea and Kensington; or a Mancunian pensioner who at 65 can expect her retirement to end nine years earlier than that of the ladies of Chelsea of the same age.

The Three Key Institutions of Inequality

Family, Capitalism and Nation are the three central institutions of contemporary inequality. They have all had their ups and downs, and while none of them is at the apogee of their institutional grip, they are currently increasing their anti-egalitarian capacity – the family in the rich world especially; capitalism everywhere, but above all because of its extension into previous state socialist and subsistence societies; and the nation worldwide because of its changed role under current globalization.

The *family* is, of course, an ancient transmission belt of inequality from one generation to the next. That role has probably diminished somewhat in modern times – although hard longitudinal evidence seems hard to find – with the diffusion of propertylessness under industrial capitalism, the generalization of formal public education, and the spread of romantic love and freedom of marriage. This process will hopefully continue in the vast remaining areas of patriarchy in the world – South Asia, Africa and rural China, above all (cf. Therborn 2004: ch. 3).

But hope will not bring about change. Movements and struggles will be required. It is a struggle for the *rights of individuals*, freely to form families, to assume family responsibilities out of moral choice, instead of through force and subservience. Northern European experience, in particular, shows that an individualistic familism is both possible and viable, manifested in high birth rates, child care, inter-generational contacts and transfers. Individualism and familism are not only conceivably compatible. They are empirically coexisting.

In the rich world, a new class homogamy[16] and a widening class gap in parenting are setting in. A consequence of the expansion and de-gendering of higher education has been that men and women with the same education marry each other. University men marry university women; high-school or drop-out women marry fellow high-school alumni or drop-outs (Schwartz and Mare 2005). For some reason, increasing class homogamy has been particularly pronounced in the UK. Between 1987 and 2004, the earnings gap between the wives of rich and of poor husbands trebled (OECD 2011a: Country Note – United Kingdom).

Marriage and bi-parental stability has become a major class divide, particularly in the USA. In 2004, 90 per cent of children of the university-educated were living with both biological parents when their mother was 40; among the parents of high-school-educated blue-collar Whites, slightly less than 30 per cent did (Murray 2012: 167; see further also McLanahan and Percheski 2008). Exactly the same pattern and tendency can be observed in Sweden, although with much less drama and trauma. In the 2000s, children's risk of parental separation has increased for those with parents without a full high-school education, while remaining stable with a slight downward tendency among children of parents with completed high-school or tertiary education (Statistics Sweden 2013a: diagram 13). Reasons are probably plentiful but one is simply age. Higher education tends to postpone coupling, and higher age of coupling favours stability (Statistics Sweden 2013b). Finally, the parents of the vastly expanded upper middle class

[16] Homogamy means likes marrying likes.

spend much more time with their children, reading to them, playing with them, taking them to ballet and music lessons and/or to various sports grounds. Most precarious blue-collar families don't do that.

What is to be done? The family is not dissolving, as some European 'individuation' sociologists, like Beck and Giddens, have argued, nor does its abolition have even the minority appeal it once had among a radical wing of Bolsheviks and *kibbutzniks*. Moralistic preaching to the wayward couples of the precarious classes may be harmless – but basically because it will not take many people very far. From an egalitarian perspective, what is important here are the life-chances of children. Sexuality, coupling and family arrangements should be left to adult individual rights to choose, but there is no reason why children should suffer from the deficiencies of their parents. And the bio-medical and psychological evidence that childhood deprivations will have life-long effects of suffering and disadvantage is piling up.

The rights of all children, to a good enabling childhood, should be a principal political guideline. This is not an extremist demand. It can refer to the UN Convention on the Rights of the Child, and, in the anti-UN USA, to the programme 'No Child Left Behind', which George W. Bush launched with the support of Edward Kennedy. It doesn't interfere with middle-class psychic and time investments in their children, but it would entail restrictions on 'freedom of choice' of exclusivist schools, and it would mean massive public investments in approximation measures to give children from disadvantaged family backgrounds a fair chance, which would imply a re-direction of public education priorities. Rights for all children will require generalized preschool child care in the rich countries, and a massive upgrading of the quality of public schools, which in most Third World countries, and in many deprived areas of the rich world, is abysmal. In India, in South Asia generally, and in much of sub-Saharan Africa, the stunting and wasting of children by malnutrition must be ended.

Capitalism is the second key generator of contemporary inequality. And it is also going to stay, for the foreseeable future. It divides people into property-owners, property-less workers and, increasingly in recent times, the unemployed – distancing people, excluding or subordinating many, and exploiting the labour of others, as well as our common environment. Its inherent ripping asunder of any social fabric is currently gaining a new dimension, the drive towards a social 'precariat' in permanently insecure and marginal employment (Standing 2011). Its competitive urge to create winners and losers is significantly adding to premature death. As we noticed above, the restoration of capitalism in the Soviet Union, under the most peaceful and favourable circumstances imaginable, cost about 4 million excess deaths in a decade.

Yet experience shows that capitalism and capitalists can, under certain circumstances, be taught how to behave. As we also noticed above, income inequality in capitalist Scandinavia around 1980 was comparable to that in the best countries of the Communist bloc. And by that time existential gender inequality was clearly lower in Scandinavia than anywhere else. Even in the USA, there is public redistribution, as we have seen above, and even under plutocratic dictat-ship, American partisan politics has made differences (cf. Bartels 2008: 62).

Against the forces of capitalism, egalitarians will have to assert two kinds of rights, *rights of labour* and *rights of citizens*. Rights of labour include what the ILO is calling the right to decent work, safe working conditions, decent pay and decent treatment (cf. Lee and McCann 2011). In the Third World, a major aspect would be extending the so-called 'formal sector' of the economy, i.e. the sector in which workers have any rights at all. It should also include the rights to form unions, to collective bargaining and to workplace consultation. These rights should be protected by decency, anti-discrimination and freedom of association laws.

A crucial labour right is also the right *to* labour – the right to a job, to a non-precarious livelihood. Once upon a time, the development of industrial capitalism meant a draining of the poverty pool of the rural landless and of the urban margins of casual labourers and hawkers. Central de-industrialization has meant a return of an 'underclass'. This is a phenomenon not only of economic significance. It is also tied up with the dysfunctionality and instability of poor families in rich countries – in the US and, very secondly, the UK, in particular. Right-wing moralists like Charles Murray have portrayed this as a decline of blue-collar 'industriousness', fostered by social liberal 'welfare' benefits. On this American issue, Murray's main opponent is the great Chicago sociologist William Julius Wilson. As a social scientist, Wilson is trained to look at structural changes of options before blaming the victims. Wilson (1987: 73) has long argued that 'male joblessness' is 'the single most important factor underlying the rise of unwed mothers among black women'.

The fact is that developed capitalist labour markets can be, and are, organized very differently from each other, with vast differences in labour force participation and in unemployment. In the crises of the 1970s, 1980s and late 2000s, unemployment outcomes varied greatly, and not according to economic growth performance, but to patterns of labour market institutionalization (Therborn 1985, 2012b). Rights of labour have to include a supply of at least minimally decent jobs, to prevent the return of a social pool of eternal poverty and despair.

Asserting the rights of citizens means, first of all, a vigorous defence of democracy, of people's right to self-determination. Citizens have a right to assert their collective will regarding their economy and their environment over any private capital interests, or any anonymous global aggregation of, e.g., financial markets. The ongoing 2008 crisis, caused by an absence of any civic control over the opulent little world of reckless speculators and high-stake casino-gamblers, acted out more in Europe than in America, is the costliest defeat of the North Atlantic democracies since the German crash of 1931–3.

Citizens' rights do stand a fair chance of regulating capitalism. Troubling to anti-egalitarian liberals is that, relatively and modestly, egalitarian capitalism has proved itself eminently competitive on the world market. The post-World War II global success of Northeast Asian capitalism, in Japan, South Korea and Taiwan, was the first, and the most spectacular, example. In the last decades, the distinguished capitalist institution of the World Management – now World Economic – Forum, organizing the annual Davos encounters, has put out a yearly *Global Competitiveness Report*. Over the years, it has been recurrently awarding top positions to all the Nordic welfare states. In the latest report (World Economic Forum 2012: 14), five of the most competitive nations, by impeccable capitalist criteria, are among the world's least unequal nations,[17] Switzerland (ranked 1st), Finland (3), Sweden (4), the Netherlands (5), Germany (6). With them are Singapore (2), the USA (7), the UK (8), Hong Kong (9) and Japan (10). In the top competitive set are also the world's two most unionized economies, of Sweden and Finland.

---

[17] All with a Gini coefficient not above 30 (or 0.3) according to the Luxemburg Income Study (www.lisproject.org).

Citizens' rights – to collective democracy, to economic and social regulation by popular self-determination, and to individual social rights to life-course development, from childhood possibilities to pensions and old-age care – were classical progressive gains of the first half of the twentieth century, boosted by Scandinavian Social Democracy, theorized in the UK by T. H. Marshall, and institutionalized in part in the US Social Security Act of 1935. But recently they have come under attack almost everywhere in the rich world, even in Scandinavia, where the citizen is increasingly relegated to the backseat, in favour of the choice-making solvent consumer and the entrepreneurial investor in him/herself.

A century ago, it was held 'a shame and a spot on the banner of Sweden, that citizenship right is called money'. It has become again, to some extent, in currently bourgeois-governed Sweden.

Vindicating labour and citizens' rights in the face of capitalism is a sine qua non of any advance towards reducing inequality. That it has to be fought for again in the core of capitalism shows that it is not utopian – because rights have before been advanced and inequality reduced – but also how much ground has been lost since 1980. In Latin America and in Asia, on the other hand, the principle of citizens' rights, and to some extent also of labour rights, is gaining ground – from a rather low starting-point, though.

The *nation* was once an institution of equality, from the American and the French Revolutions, even founding a slightly egalitarian counter-revolutionary current of One Nation Toryism, from Benjamin Disraeli to R. A. B. Butler and Harold Macmillan. Post-World War II national development projects often had a substantial, not only rhetorical, egalitarian component, in the export-oriented Northeast Asian take-off as well as in the inward-oriented import substitution model of

Argentine Peronism. Under post-1990 globalization, however, national cohesion and equality have been dumped for national attractiveness to foreign capital, in China and Vietnam as well as in Argentina, Eastern Europe and elsewhere. In this way, nations have become territories of cheap bodies, pimped by their elites to foreign capital, and as such almost unprecedented generators of inequality.

Nations and national boundaries still matter a lot under current globalization, but nowadays largely as institutions of inequality. They provide the national pimp governments with their exorbitant rents, and they constitute major barriers of exclusion to poor migrants. Nations are not being overtaken or submerged by 'cosmopolitan' upper- and upper-middle-class people. The UN has almost quadrupled its number of members since its beginning, and the demand for nation-statehood is continuing: from Palestine, Kossovo, Abchazia, Kurdistan, Catalonia, Québec, Scotland and so on.

The legitimacy of nations and nation-states is inscribed in modernity, and futile to deny. But there has to be an assertion of a superior *right of all humans*. A right to universal migration is not on any practical agenda. A 'cosmopolitan' right for everybody with a certain, high, amount of wealth, or with extraordinary professional qualifications, would not add to world equality, and at least the former – the more common one – would reduce it. Ageing rich countries urgently need immigrants, and the Japanese are self-defeatingly narrow-minded in not recognizing it. The egalitarian task is not primarily to regulate the extent of international migration, but to ensure that all immigrants get a fair deal.

The institution of the nation itself has to be reformed. The contemporary extensively and intensely connected world, with its irresistible flows of communication, of trade and of people, has made the classical, cohesive 'imagined community' nation unviable. Recent attempts to reinforce it, by proclamations of national identity, by national culture definitions, through culture tests – to which the liberal Dutch have added a soft-porn topless accent in order to provoke Muslim bigots – etc., are no more than defensive rearguard actions. For related, if not exactly the same, reasons, the twentieth-century project of 'national development' has also largely been overtaken by current globalized capitalism. At the same time, the nation is, or at least can be, a resource to most people of the world.

There is a need for what might be called a concept of the *civilian nation*: a human collective living together in a common civility, on a contingently bounded terri-tory – with its distinctive geography and its contingent history. A civility, not only tolerating its members letting their capabilities flourish, but collectively committed to supporting and promoting those capabilities in their vital, existential and resource aspects.

For the foreseeable future, nations remain indispen-sable for human rights. However, the rights of all humans have, of course, first of all, a planetary dimen-sion, referring to a concern with the life-chances of the species. Here, the human vision is often blurred and deliberately distorted by imperial and national powers. Human rights have been and still are ideologically instrumentalized by imperial powers, motivating sanc-tions, blockades and military invasions against national/imperial enemies, pushing the rest of the world out of the spotlight. But the basic meaning of the rights of all humans is the right to survival, to develop one's human capability, and to use that capability at one's own choice. What to look at, and to heed, is not the compilations of imperial institutions like the US State Department or 'Freedom House', but the UN *Human Development Reports*. Implementing the simple demand of equal human rights for all would then be seen as involving a major global transformation.

Egalitarians will have to find ways to confront and to overcome these three institutional challenges. They will also have to win a crucial social battle.

The Decisive Battle – For the Orientation of the Middle Classes

The twentieth century was *the* century of the working class, when it reached its peak of cultural centrality – recognized already in 1891 by the Papal Encyclica *Rerum Novarum (On New Things)* – and of its economic and political clout (see further Therborn 2012a). The working class of the twentieth century never and nowhere became large and strong enough to dictate a programme of social change. The big Scandinavian labour success was possible, first because of the 1930s alignment with the propertied farmers, and second, in the 1950s, because of an alliance with the white-collar salariat. Both operations required a large amount of political and, in the latter case, also actuarial skill (making a white-collar opt-out of the public occupational insurance scheme unattractive). Nevertheless, in the European history of egalitarianism, the working class was the central actor, and its possibilities were largely determined by the tactical and managerial skills of the leaders of the labour movement.

With the structural decline of the industrial working class in the core areas of capitalism, and its still remaining weakness in the developing world, the social parameters of possible egalitarianism shift. While labour remains important, both as a force and as a social compass, in the next coming years the chances of equality will hinge primarily not on the strength of the labour movements and the skills of its leadership, but on the orientation of the Middle Classes.

In recent years there has been an avalanche of discourses, papers and competing statistics on the middle class(es). For the time being, this is a phenomenon to be studied, rather than trying a call to order by a hopeless attempt at conceptual rigour in class definition. Basically, the 'middle class' refers to the non-rich and the non-poor, without necessarily any social characteristics other than consumerism, although sometimes a cultural or policy orientation is implied.

There are two predominant types of middle-class discourse – one, concentrated in the USA, echoed in the UK, where the upper middle class is always tuned in to the Voice of America. This variant is *larmoyant* in tone and critical in intent. It talks about 'the suffering middle classes', as BBC's Europe Editor Gavin Hewitt put it on 25 January 2012. Well before that (*Financial Times*, 30 July 2010), the *FT* Washington Bureau Chief, Edward Luce, wrote about 'The crisis of middle class America'. In *Time* (10 October 2011), Jeffrey Sachs, once a neoliberal crusader leaving heavy footprints of escalating inequality from Bolivia to Russia, weighed in with a passionate call: 'Why America Must Revive Its Middle Class'. Repentant sinners should of course be forgiven, and, in its own peculiar sense, this concern with the suffering North Atlantic middle classes who are left behind the soaring oligarchy of current financial capitalism is a critical concern with inequality, to be welcomed by all egalitarians. That inequality is seen in mainstream media through the prism of the middle class is a noteworthy sign of our new century.

The other middle-class discourse prevailing in and about the rest of the world is opposite in tone, jubilant, telling about the arrival or the imminent coming of the Messiah, in the shape of consuming middle classes. As you would expect, this annunciation is spread first of all by business consultancies – McKinsey, the Boston Consulting Group and all the lesser stars. (A conveniently brief overview is given by Pilling et al. 2011.) But it has also been taken up by a growing number of public economic agencies. At the OECD, the Director of its Development Centre is hailing 'an emerging middle class' (Pezzini 2012; cf. Kharas 2010). The Asian Development Bank is understandably paying considerable attention to the rising middle class of its continent (e.g. Chun 2010); somewhat less self-evidently, the African Development Bank (2011) is doing the same. Even such a serious development economist as Nancy Birdsall (2010) is talking, with a parenthetical caveat, of 'the (indispensable) Middle Class'.

The middle class in this discourse variant, obviously inspired by the recent growth of Asian, African and Latin American economies, is envisaged as a growing consumer pool – of cars and other consumer durables, above all – for profitable business, as a reason for a macroeconomic re-orientation from mainly export-driven growth to one with some reliance on domestic consumption. The middle class is also portrayed as the social basis of 'sound economics' and, in the most naïve or ideologically blinded versions, as a 'bulwark of democracy', as if the successful bloody middle-class coup in Chile in 1973, the abortive coup in Venezuela in 2002, and the Yellow Shirts rebellion in Thailand in 2008 had never taken place.

Chinese social science intellectuals have recently become enthralled with middle class prospects, with benevolent intentions, seeing a middle-class society as an 'olive-shaped' alternative to the social pyramid of the imperial tradition (Zhou Xiaohong 2008; Li Chunling 2012) – a lofty goal, though usually discreetly leaving out that it is precisely current 'middle-class' China which has made the country one of the most unequal in Asia. An olive-shaped resource distribution was actually proclaimed a governmental aim of the Chinese State Council in February 2013, but without any concrete road map (*China Daily – European Weekly*, 8–14 March 2013, p. 8).

A few serious economists of distribution, like Martin Ravaillon (2010) of the World Bank and Ricardo Paez de Barros in Brazil, are seeing the emergent middle class more as a still 'vulnerable' adolescent.

It is in this new 'middle-class' century that egalitarians will have to move. The vagueness of the class concept and its widely varying size estimates are not primarily important. We are dealing with classes of people, non-poor and non-rich, without any other overriding social identity – as workers, farmers, professionals. They are currently called to possess the earth. The President of Brazil, the former *guerrillera* Dilma Roussef, desires to 'transform Brazil into a middle-class population'.[18] At the World Economic Forum on East Asia in 2009, the deputy prime minister of the Communist Party state of Vietnam, Mr Huang Trung Hai, declared: 'The young middle-class population will be the driving force in Asian countries' (www.weforum.org/news/asian-middle-class-drive-growth). Not so long ago, but in the past century, his teachers no doubt told him that the working class would be the driver of (at least) Vietnamese development.

It is in this middle-class world that the fight for equality will have to be fought. In the US it will be natural, and wise, to tag on to current middle-class lamentation and, above all, anger at the oligarchy which has abandoned them. But the future of inequality in the world will hardly be decided in North America, or Western Europe. It will be in Asia, in Latin America and in Africa.

[18] Jaim Leahy, 'FT interview: Dilma Roussef', *Financial Times*, 3 October 2012.

Fortunately, it will not be decided inside the middle class alone, but across a wide social spectrum. The new working class of China has already become restive, and the Indonesian or Bangladeshi working class is likely to do so tomorrow. In Latin America, the 'people of colour' are refusing to accept the conditions of coloniality, and the popular classes are entering the centre stage in several countries, from parts of Central America and from Venezuela to Bolivia. In the rich world, the Occupy and the Education movements, from the Mediterranean to the Americas, and there from Québec to Chile, show that people are no longer taking the world of financial capitalism lying down. The World Social Fora (in 2013 in Tunis) are bringing the world's social movements together. The social heat on the rising middle classes is already on. To all egalitarians, it should be clear that, without the movements and the struggles of the 'people', i.e., of those who don't see themselves as above the poor, the crucial battle for the orientation of the middle classes is doomed in advance.

Third-World middle-class hubris, which is of course a principal aim of the business consultants, the transnational corporations and their intellectual courtiers, will be a main problem. The US liberal middle-class myth of modern capitalist history, which has so captivated today's Chinese academics, has to be subjected to the deconstruction of *Ideologiekritik*, demonstrating its deliberate distortion of nineteenth- and twentieth-century American and European history, blotting out the struggles and the movements of workers, farmers, ethnic minorities, and women *qua* women, and ignoring the narrow-minded viciousness of significant parts of the urban middle class, supplying strike-breakers, lynch mobs and anti-tax revolts. Left to their middle classes alone, neither the USA nor Western Europe would have reached universal suffrage when they did, if ever (see further Therborn 1977). Nor would there have been any Western welfare state.

Current Chinese middle-class discourse has, of course, to be viewed against the traumatic experiences of the Maoist concepts of people and of class conflict, and as a repudiation of them. Important here is not an acceptance of an alternative popular-democratic narrative of modern history, only a scepticism towards the ideology of modernity as middle-class only. Because the crucial political problem of the twenty-first century will be to connect a sizeable part of the middle class with the people, or to get part of the former to see itself as part of, not as the substitute for, the latter. The irony of some middle-class idealizations has not been lost on cool Chinese analysts. Referring to a prominent Chinese academic definition of a 'middle-class society', as involving, among other criteria, a Gini coefficient between 0.25 and 0.30, Zhou Xiaohong (2008: 113) points out that then the USA would not qualify.

On the other hand, the shining admiration of the middle class in the US and in today's China is not replicated everywhere. Particularly in India, there is a refreshing critical discussion going on, including the writer Parwan Varma's (1998: 174) famous diatribe against 'the Great Indian Middle Class' as 'morally rudderless, obsessively materialistic, and socially insensitive'. In a more cautious scholarly language, Leela Fernandes (2006: 214) has emphasized 'the emergence of a new middle class model of consumer-citizenship that has sought to rework social exclusions as a new form of civic life that draws on discourses of consumption and privatization'.

For affluent consumers in Western Europe and North America (including Cambridge academics), it would be a ridiculous hollowness to sermonize, *extra muros*, of the dangers of consumerism. Some gentle pointing to the hard local evidence of costs already in existence – of, for example, pollution in Beijing and Delhi, or Jakarta and São Paolo traffic jams – should not be taken as patronizingly offensive, though.

There are at least three kinds of arguments – apart from accommodating to the probable accumulation of popular forces – which egalitarians may put to the triumphant middle classes in favour of an alignment with the people, rather than with a pursuit of maximizing personal consumption.

One is the social cost of other people's misery. Few people actually take pleasure in other people's suffering. Without support from any representative-sample surveys, I would venture the proposition that most middle-class Kolkatans, Cairenes, Kinois, Angelenos or Paulistas would prefer to walk (or drive) the cities of, say, Paris or Stockholm, where they will not get confronted with abject misery, where streets and public spaces are clean – not because the miserable have been chased away, but because society itself is cleaned of abject misery. Most middle-class people are likely to be happier without walled-in seclusion, barbed wire and armed bodyguards, without whom the happy middle classes of Northwestern Europe are living.

The second is the illegitimacy, from a middle-class viewpoint, of the ruthless exclusivism of the oligarchs of financial and rent capitalism, today's parasitic equivalents to the aristocracy facing the French Revolution 'Third Estate' or middle class. The oligarchy from Wall Street New York to post-Soviet Moscow, from Shanghai to Lagos and Mexico, whose wealth stems not from hard productive work, thrift and honest exchange, but from connections – parental and/or political – from gambling and from sidestepping existing norms and regulations, has cut itself off from the middle class, not only in wealth, but, above all, in behaviour. It was a common revulsion against this oligarchy which in 2011 brought together the pan-Mediterranean protest movements, of the middle and the popular classes, and also moved the established middle-class parents onto the same streets as their student or unemployed sons and daughters. The oligarchs, the One Per Cent, have let the middle classes down, and 'the people' are getting restive, and likely to grow in force, at least in Africa, Asia and Latin America. Opting for exclusivist middle-class consumerism, instead of some alignment with the people, is a risky bet.

The third argument would invoke the Elysian Fields of Freedom and Human Rationality, or, put more prosaically, the positive lure of enlightened societies governed by rational and inclusive deliberation, where nobody is outcast or humiliated, and where everybody has a chance to develop his/her capabilities. If there is any truth in the classical middle-class self-image of autonomy, rationality and responsibility, then an egalitarian enlightened society would be an excellent site for its realization.

The battle is about to start. Nobody knows how it will end. Which side will you be on?

References

African Development Bank 2011. 'The middle of the pyramid: dynamics of the middle class in Africa', www.afdb.org

African Statistical Yearbook 2012 www.uneca.org

Allen, R. C. 2005. 'Real wages in Europe and Asia: a first look at long-term patterns', in R. C. Allen and T. Bengtsson (eds.) *Living Standards in the Past*. Oxford: Oxford University Press

Almquist, Y. 2011. *A Class of Origin: The School Class as a Social Context and Health Disparities in a Life-course Perspective*. Stockholm University, Department of Sociology, Ph.D. thesis

Asian Development Bank 2012a. 'Regional trends and associations of outcome indicators with indicators of policy pillars and good governance', www.adb.org/data/statistics

Asian Development Bank 2012b. 'Asian development outlook 2012', www.adb.org

Atkinson, A. and Bourguignon, F. (eds.) 2000. *Handbook of Income Distribution*. Amsterdam: Elsevier

Atkinson, A. and Piketty, T. (eds.) 2010. *Top Incomes: A Global Perspective*. Oxford: Oxford University Press

Atkinson, A., Piketty, T. and Saez, E. 2010. 'Top incomes in the long run of history', pp. 664–759 in A. Atkinson and

T. Piketty (eds.) *Top Incomes in Global Perspective*. Oxford: Oxford University Press

Banda, F. 2008. 'Women, law and human rights: an African perspective'. London: SOAS research online, http://eprints.soas.ac.uk/id/eprint/3426

Bartels, L. 2008. *Unequal Democracy*. Princeton: Princeton University Press

Berman, G. 2012. 'The cost of international military operations', www.parliament.uk/briefing-papers/SN03139

Bethune, A. 1997. 'Unemployment and mortality', ch. 12 in F. Drever and M. Whitehead (eds.) *Health Inequalities*. London: Office of National Statistics

Bhandari, P. forthcoming (2013). 'Spouse-selection in New Delhi: a study of upper middle-class marriages', Cambridge University, Department of Sociology, Ph.D. thesis

Bilger, M. and Carrien, V. 2013. 'Health in the cities: when the neighbourhood makes more than income', *Journal of Health Economics* 32(1): 1–11

Birdsall, N. 2010. 'The (indispensable) middle class in developing countries', Washington DC, Center for Global Development Working Paper 207

Björklund, A. and Jäntti, M. 2011. *Inkomstfördelningen i Sverige*. Stockholm: SNS

Blackburn, R. 2011. *The American Crucible*. London: Verso

Boltanski, L. and Chiapello, E. 2007 *The New Spirit of Capitalism*. Cambridge: Polity

Bourdieu, P. 1979. *La distinction*. Paris: Ed. de Minuit

Breen, R., et al. 2009. 'Nonpersistent inequality in educational attainment: evidence from eight European countries', *American Journal of Sociology* 114(5): 1–39

Brewer, M., Browne, J. and Joyce, R. 2011. *Child and Working Age Poverty from 2010 to 2020*. London: Institute for Fiscal Studies

Brown, W., et al. 2009. *The Evolution of the Modern Workplace*. Cambridge: Cambridge University Press

Case, A. and Paxson, C. 2008. 'Status and Statute: Height, Ability, and Labor Market Outcomes', *Journal of Political Economy* 116(5): 499–532

Castells, M. 1998. *The Rise of the Network Society*. Oxford: Blackwell

Castells, M. 2012. *Networks of Outrage and Hope.* Cambridge: Polity

CEPAL 2010. *La hora de igualdad.* Santiago de Chile: CEPAL. [CEPAL is the acronym in Spanish for the UN's Economic Commission for Latin America and the Caribbean]

CEPAL 2011. *Panorama social de América Latina 2011.* Santiago de Chile: CEPAL

CEPAL 2012. *Social Panorama of Latin America 2012.* Santiago de Chile: CEPAL

Chang, Jung 1991. *Wild Swans.* London: Flamingo

Charsley, K. and Shaw, A. 2006. 'South Asian transnational marriages in comparative perspective', *Global Networks* 6(4): 331–44

Chua, A. 2003. *World on Fire.* London: William Heinemann

Chun, N. 2010. 'Middle class size in the past, present and future: a description of trends in Asia', Asia Development Bank Working Paper 217, www.adb.org

Congressional Budget Office 2011a. *Trends in the Distribution of Household Income between 1979 and 2007.* Washington DC: Congressional Budget Office

Congressional Budget Office 2011b. *Changes in the Distribution of Workers' Hourly Wages between 1979 and 2009.* Washington DC: Congressional Budget Office

Corak, M. 2012. 'Social mobility and social institutions: Canada in international perspective', CSLS presentation 20 September 2012, www.csls.ca/presentations

Cornia, G. A. (ed.) 2004. *Inequality, Growth, and Poverty in an Era of Liberalization and Globalization.* Oxford: Oxford University Press

Cornia, G. A., Addison, T. and Kiiski, S. 2004. 'Income Distribution Changes and Their Impact in the Post Second World War Period', pp. 26–54 in G. A. Cornia (ed.) *Inequality, Growth, and Poverty in an Era of Liberalization and Globalization.* Oxford: Oxford University Press

Cornia, G. A. and Menchini, L. 2006. 'Health improvements and health inequality during 40 years', Helsinki UNU-Wider, UNU-Wider Research Paper 2006/10

Conia, G. A. and Paniccià, R. 2000. 'The transition mortality crisis: evidence, interpretation and policy responses', pp. 3–37 in Conia and Paniccià (eds.) *The Mortality Crisis in Transitional Economies*. Oxford: Oxford University Press

Crouch, C. 2011. *The Strange Non-Death of Neoliberalism*. Cambridge: Polity

Danmarks Statistik 2011. Indkomster 2010, www.dst.dk

Das, P. 2012. 'Wage inequality in India', *Economic and Political Weekly* 15 December, pp. 58–64

Deaton, A. 2008. 'Height, weight, and inequality: the distribution of adult heights in India', *American Economic Review* 88(2): 468–74

Dempsey, J. 2013. 'Greek forces spared from deep cuts', *International Herald Tribune* 8 January, p. 2

Deng Quheng, Gustafsson, B. and Li Shi 2012. 'Intergenerational income persistence in urban China', Bonn IZA Discussion Paper 6907, iza@iza.org

Department for Work and Pensions 2012. 'Households below average income: an analysis of the income distribution 1994/95–2010/11', www.dpw.gov.uk

The Economist 2012. Special Report: World Economy. 13 October

Eibner, C. and Evans, W. 2005. 'Relative deprivation, poor health habits, and mortality', *Journal of Human Resources* 40(3): 591–620

Elo, I. 2009. 'Social class differentials in health and mortality: patterns and explanations in comparative perspective', *Annual Review of Sociology* 35: 553–72

Eriksson, R. and Goldthorpe, J. 1992. *The Constant Flux*. Oxford: Clarendon Press

European Societies 2012. Special issue on 'Antisemitism and Racism', 14(2)

Eurostat 2013. http://epp.eurostat.ec.europa.eu, accessed 29 January 2013

Evans, W., Wolfe, B. and Adler, N. 2012. 'The SES and the health gradient: a brief review of the literature', pp. 38–62 in B. Wolfe, W. Evans and T. Seeman (eds.) *The Biological Consequences of Socioeconomic Inequalities*. New York: Russell Sage Foundation

Fernandes, L. 2006. *India's New Middle Class*. Minneapolis and London: University of Minnesota Press

Ferreira, F. and Gignoux, J. 2011. 'The measurement of inequality of opportunity: theory and an application to Latin America', *Income and Wealth* 57(4): 622–56

Fitzpatrick, R. and Chandola, T. 2000. 'Health', pp. 94–127 in A. H. Halsey (ed.) *British Social Trends*. Basingstoke: Macmillan

Floud, R., et al. 2011. *The Changing Body*. Cambridge: Cambridge University Press

Fogel, R. 2012. *Evolving Long-Term Trends in Health and Longevity*. Cambridge: Cambridge University Press

Frank, J. 2013. *Ike and Dick: Portrait of a Strange Political Marriage*. New York: Simon & Schuster

Fraser, N. and Honneth, A. 2003. *Redistribution or Recognition?* London: Verso

Frijters, P., et al. 2009. 'Childhood economic conditions and length of life: evidence from the British Boyd–Orr cohort, 1937–2005', *Journal of Health Economics* 29: 39–47

Galanter, M. 1984. *Competing Equalities*. Delhi: Oxford University Press

Gerdtham, U. G. and Johannesson, M. 2003. 'A note on the effect of unemployment on mortality', *Journal of Health Economics* 22(3): 505–18

Gerschenkron, A. 1962. *Economic Backwardness in Historical Perspective*. Cambridge MA: Belknap / Harvard University Press

Gilens, M. 2012. *Affluence and Influence*. New York and Princeton: Russell Sage Foundation and Princeton University Press

Glendon, M. A. 2001. *The World Made New*. New York: Random House

Goesling, B. and Baker, D. 2008. 'Three faces of international inequality', *Research in Social Stratification and Mobility* 26: 183–96

Goos, M., Manning, A., Salomons, A. 2009. 'Job polarization in Europe', *American Economic Review: Papers and Proceedings* 99(2): 58–63

Grant, J. (ed.) 1968. *Black Protest* Greenwich, CT: Fawcett

Grimm, M., et al. 2009. 'Inequality in human development: an empirical assessment of 32 countries', Luxemburg Income Study Working Paper 519, www.lisproject.org

Hacker, A. 2012. 'We're More Unequal Than You Think', *New York Review of Books* 59(3): 34–6

Hacker, J. and Pierson, P. 2010. *Winner-Take-All Politics*. New York: Simon & Schuster

Hanlon, P., Walsh, D. and Whyte, B. 2008. *Let Glasgow Flourish*. Glasgow: Centre for Population Health

Hastings, M. 2012. *The Operators: The Wild and Terrifying Story of America's War in Afghanistan*. New York: Blue Rider

Hewitt, G. 2012. 'The suffering middle classes', *BBC World News* 25 January, www. bbc.co.uk/news/world-europe

Hout, M. and DiPrete, T. 2006. 'What we have learned: RC28's contribution to knowledge about social stratification', *Research in Social Stratification and Mobility* 124: 1–20

Houweling, T., and Kunst, A. 2009. 'Socioeconomic inequalities in childhood mortality in low and middle-income countries: a review of the international evidence', *British Medical Bulletin* 93: 7–26

ILO 2010. *Global Employment Trends*. Geneva: ILO

Inglehart, R. and Norris, P. 2004. *Rising Tide*. Cambridge: Cambridge University Press

Inglehart, R, et al. (eds.) 2003. *Human Beliefs and Values*. Mexico: Siglo XXI

Jäntti, M., et al. 2006. 'American exceptionalism in a new light: a comparison of intergenerational earnings mobility in the Nordic countries, the United Kingdom and the United States', IZA Discussion Paper 1938, http://ftp.iza.org

Jones, G. 2010. 'Changing marriage patterns in Asia', Singapore: Asia Research Institute Working Paper 131, arigwj@nus.edu.sg

Jones, O. 2011. *Chavs*. London: Verso

Judd, E. R. 2010. 'Family strategies: fluidities of gender, community and mobility in rural West China', *China Quarterly* 204: 927–38

Kaplan, S. and Rauh, J. 2007. 'Wall Street and Main Street: what contributes to the rise of the highest incomes?' National Bureau of Economic Research Working Paper 13270, www.nber.org/papers

Karasek, R. and Theorell, T. 1990. *Healthy Work: Stress, Productivity, and the Reconstruction of Working Life*. New York: Basic Books

Kelly, N. 2009. *The Politics of Income Inequality in the United States*. Cambridge: Cambridge University Press

Kharas, H. 2010. 'The emerging middle class in developing countries', OECD Development Centre Working Paper 285, www.oecd.org

Kivinen, M. and Li Chunling 2012 'The free market or the welfare state?' pp. 47–113 in C. Pursiainen (ed.) *At the Crossroads of Post-Communist Modernization*. Basingstoke: Palgrave Macmillan

Korpi, W. 1983. *The Democratic Class Struggle*. London: Routledge

Kunst, A. 1997. 'Cross-national comparisons of socio-economic differences in mortality', Rotterdam, Erasmus University, Department of Health, thesis

Kuznets, S. 1955. 'Economic growth and inequality', *American Economic Review* 45: 1–28

Lazarsfeld, P. and Rosenberg, M. (eds.) 1955 *The Language of Social Research*. New York: The Free Press

Lee, S. and McCann, D. 2011. *Regulating for Decent Work*. Basingstoke: Palgrave Macmillan and ILO

Lefranc, A., Pistolesi, N. and Trannoy, A. 2008. 'Inequality of opportunity vs. inequality of outcomes: are Western societies all alike?' *Review of Income and Wealth* 54(4): 513–44

Leibbrandt, M., et al. 2010. 'Trends in South African income distribution and poverty since the fall of apartheid', OECD Social Employment and Migration Working Paper 101, http//: dx.doi.org/10.1787

Leinsalu, M., et al. 2009. 'Educational inequalities in mortality in four Eastern European countries: divergence in trends during the post-communist transition from 1990 to 2000', *International Journal of Epidemiology* 38. 512–25

Lenski, G. 1966. *Power and Privilege*. New York: McGraw-Hill

Li Chunling (ed.) (2012) *The Rising Middle Classes of China*. Beijing and London: Social Sciences Academic Press and Paths International

Li Shi, Luo Chiang and T. Sicular 2011. 'Overview: income inequality and poverty in China, 2002–2007', www.iza. org/conference/files/CIER 2011/ li_s161

Lindahl, M., et al. 2012. 'The intergenerational persistence of human capital: an empirical analysis of four generations', *IZA* Discussion Paper 6463, www.iza.org

Lindert, P. 2000. 'Three centuries of inequality in Britain and America', pp. 167–216 in A. Atkinson and F. Bourguignon (eds.) *Handbook of Income Distribution*, Vol. I. Amsterdam: Elsevier

Lipset, S. M. and Smelser, N. (eds.) 1961, *Sociology: The Progress of A Decade*. Englewood Cliffs NJ: Prentice-Hall

Livi-Bacci, M. 1993. 'On the human costs of collectivization in the Soviet Union', *Population and Development Review* 19(4): 743–66

Livi-Bacci, M. 2000. 'Mortality crises in a historical perspective: the European experience', pp. 38–58 in G. A. Cornia and R. Paniccià (eds.) *The Mortality Crisis in Transitional Economies*. Oxford: Oxford University Press

London Health Observatory 2011. *Capital Health Gains?* www.lho.org.uk

Luce, E. 2010. 'The crisis of middle class America', *Financial Times* 30 July, www.ft.com

Lustig, N., et al. 2012a. 'The impact of taxes and social spending on inequality and poverty in Argentina, Bolivia, Brazil, Mexico, and Peru: a synthesis of results', Tulane University, Tulane Economics Working Paper 1216

Lustig, N., et al. 2012b. 'Declining inequality in Latin America in the 2000s: the cases of Argentina. Brazil, and Mexico', ECINEQ Working Paper 2012-266, www.ecineq. orgG68

Luxemburg Income Study 2012. 'Key figures of inequality' www.lisproject.org

McLanahan, S. and Percheski, C. 2008. 'Family structure and the reproduction of inequalities', *Annual Review of Sociology* 34: 257–76

Mackenbach, J., et al. 1997. 'Socioeconomic inequalities in morbidity and mortality in Western Europe', *The Lancet* 349: 1655–9

Mackenbach, J., et al. 2008. 'Socioeconomic inequalities in health in 22 European countries', *New England Journal of Medicine* 358: 2468–81

Maddison, A. 2001. *The World Economy: A Millennial Perspective.* Paris: OECD

Maddison, A. 2007. *Contours of the World Economy, 1-2030 A.D.* Oxford: Oxford University Press

Marmot, M. 2004. *Status Syndrome.* London: Bloomsbury

Marmot, M. 2012. 'Two years on', UCL Institute of Health Equity, http://marmot-reviewblogspot.copm/2012

Marmot, M. and Bobak, M. 2000. 'Psychosocial and biological mechanisms behind the recent mortality crisis in Central and Eastern Europe', pp. 127–48 in G. A. Cornia and R. Paniccià (eds.) *The Mortality Crisis in Transition Economies.* Oxford: Oxford University Press

Marrero, G. and Rodríguez, J. G. 2012. 'Inequality of Opportunity in Europe', *Review of Income and Wealth* 58(4): 597–620

Marx, K. 1875/1969. *Kritik des Gothaer Programms. Marx-Engels-Werke*, Vol. XIX. East Berlin: Dietz

Mason, P. 2012. *Why It's Kicking Off Everywhere.* London: Verso

Mayer, A. 1981. *The Persistence of the Old Régimes.* London: Croom Helm

Milanovic, B. 2005. *Worlds Apart.* Princeton: Princeton University Press

Milanovic, B. 2012. 'Global income inequality by the numbers: in history and now', World Bank Policy Research Working Paper 6259

Milburn, A. 2012. 'Fair access to professional careers: a progress report', www.gov.uk

Milburn, A., et al. 2009. 'Unleashing aspiration: the final report on the Panel of Fair Access to the Professions', www.webarchive.nationalarchives.gov.uk

Mishel, L., Bernstein, J. and Shierholz, H. 2009. *The State of Working America 2008/2009.* Ithaca and London: ILR Press

Mishel, L., Schmitt, J. and Shierholz, H. 2013. 'Assessing the job polarization explanation of wage inequality',

Economic Policy Institute Working Paper 295, www.epi. org/publications

Mitchell, B. R. 1998. *International Historical Statistics: The Americas*, 4th edn. London: Macmillan

Mody, P. 2008. *The Intimate State: Love Marriage and the Law in Delhi*. New Delhi: Routledge

Moser, K. A., Fox, A. J. and Jones, D. R. 1994. 'Unemployment and mortality in the OPCS longitudinal study', in A. Steptoe and J. Wardle (eds.) *Psychosocial Processes and Health: A Reader, 12*. Cambridge: Cambridge University Press

Mosley, L. 2011. *Labor Rights and Multinational Corporations*. Cambridge: Cambridge University Press

Morrisson, C. 2000. 'Historical perspectives on income distribution: the case of Europe', pp. 217–60 in A. Atkinson and F. Bourguignon (eds.) *Handbook of Income Distribution*. Amsterdam: Elsevier

Munroe, S. n.d. 'The persons case', http://canadaoneline. about.com/cs/women//a/personscase.htm, accessed 29 January 2013

Murray, C. 2012. *Coming Apart*. New York: Crown Forum

Namasivayam, A., et al. 2012. 'The role of gender inequities in women's access to reproductive health care: a population-level study of Namibia, Kenya, Nepal, and India', *Journal of Women's Health* 4: 351–64

Netherlands Central Bureau of Statistics 2012, release 12-031, www.cbs.nl

Noah, T. 2012. *The Great Divergence*. London and New York: Bloomsbury Press

Nussbaum, M. 2011. *Creating Capabilities*. Cambridge MA: The Belknap Press

Nylén, L., Voss, M, and Floderus, B. 2001. 'Mortality among women and men relative to unemployment, part time work, overtime work, and extra work: a study based on data from the Swedish twin registry', *Occupational and Environmental Medicine* 58(1): 52–7

Ó Gráda, C. 2009. *Famine*. Princeton: Princeton University Press

OECD 2007. *Employment Outlook 2007*. Paris: OECD, www.oecd.org

OECD 2008. *Growing Unequal?* Paris: OECD, www.oecd. org

OECD 2011a. *Divided We Stand.* Paris: OECD, www.oecd. org

OECD 2011b. *OECD at a Glance.* Paris: OECD, www.oecd. org

OECD 2012. *Perspectives on Global Development 2012.* Paris: OECD, www.oecd.org

Office of National Statistics 2010. 'Social Trends 40', www. statistics.gov.uk

Office of National Statistics 2011. 'Statistical bulletin: life expectancy at birth and at age 65 by local areas in the United Kingdom, 2004–6 to 2008–10', www.ons.gov.uk

Official Statistics of Finland 2012. Income distribution statistics, http:/tilastokeskus.fi

Olshansky, J., et al. 2012 'Differences in life expectancy due to race and educational differences are widening, and may not catch up', *Health Affairs* 31(8): 1803–10

Paquot, T. (ed.) 2009 *Ghettos de riches.* Paris: Perrin

Paugam, S. (ed.) 1996 *L'Exclusion, l'état des savoirs.* Paris: La Découverte

Penn, R. 2011. 'Arranged marriages in Western Europe: media representation and social reality', *Journal of Comparative Family Studies* 42(5): 637–50

Pezzini, M. 2012. 'An emerging middle class', *OECD Observer* 17(8), www.oecdobserver.org

Pijoan-Mas, J. and Rios-Rull, V. 2012. 'Who lives longer?' www.voxeu.org/article/who-lives-longer-and-why

Pilling, D., Hile, K. and Kazmin, A. 2011. 'Asia: the rise of the middle class', *Financial Times*, 4 January

Rablen, M. and Oswald, A. 2008. 'Mortality and immortality: the Nobel Prize as an experiment into the effect of status upon longevity', *Journal of Health Economics* 27(6): 1462–71

Rae, D., et al. 1981. *Equalities.* Cambridge MA: Harvard University Press

Rajaratnam, J. K., et al. 2010. 'Worldwide mortality in men and women aged 15–59 years from 1970 to 2010: a systematic analysis', *Lancet* 375: 1704–20

Rao, A. 2009. *The Caste Question*. Berkeley: University of California Press

Ravaillon, M. 2010., 'The developing world's bulging (but vulnerable) middle class', *World Development* 38(4): 445–54

Rawls, J. 1971. *A Theory of Justice*. Cambridge MA: Harvard University Press

Redelmeier, D. and Singh, S. 2001. 'Survival in Academy-Award winning actors and actresses', *Annals of Internal Medicine* 134(10): 955–62

Roemer, J. 1982. *A General Theory of Exploitation and Class*. Cambridge MA: Harvard University Press

Roemer, J. 1998. *Equality of Opportunity*. Cambridge MA, Harvard University Press

Roine, J. and Waldenström, D. 2012. 'On the role of capital gains in Swedish income inequality', *Review of Income and Wealth* 58(3): 569–87

Rosanvallon, P. 2011. *La société des égaux*. Paris: Seuil

Rothstein, B. and Uslaner, E. 2005. 'All for all: equality, corruption, and social trust', *World Politics* 58: 41–72

Sachs, J. 2011. 'Why America must revive its middle class', *Time* 10 December, pp. 32–3

Sandel, M. 2012. *What Money Can't Buy*. London: Allen Lane

Sassi, F. 2009. 'Health inequalities: a persistent problem', pp. 135–56 in J. Hills et al. (eds.) *Toward a More Equal Society?* Bristol: Policy Press

Schama, S. 2005. *Rough Crossings*. London: BBC Books

Schwartz, C. and Mare, R. 2005. 'Trends in educational assortative marriage from 1940 to 2003', *Demography* 42(4): 621–46

Seekings, J. and Nattrass, N. 2006. *Class, Race, and Inequality in South Africa*. Scottsville: University of Kwa-Zulu-Natal Press

Sen. A. 1992. *Inequality Reexamined*. Cambridge MA: Harvard University Press

Sen, A. 2009. *The Idea of Justice*. London: Allen Lane

Sharma, K. L. (ed.) 1994. *Caste and Class in India*. Jaipur and New Delhi: Rawat

Shavit, Y. and Blossfeld, H.-P. 1993. *Persistent Inequality: Changing Educational Attainment in Thirteen Countries.* Boulder: Westview Press

Shkolnikov, V. and Cornia, G. A. 2000. 'Population crisis and rising mortality in transitional Russia', pp. 253–79 in G. A. Cornia and R. Paniccià (eds.) *The Mortality Crisis in Transitional Economies.* Oxford: Oxford University Press

Shkolnikov, V., McKee, M. and Leon, D. 2001. 'Changes in life expectancy in Russia in the mid-1990s', *Lancet* 357: 91720

Sihvonen, A.-P. 1998. 'Socioeconomic inequalities in health expectancy in Finland and Norway in the late 1980s', *Social Science and Medicine* 47(3): 303–15

Singh, A. 2012. 'Inequality of opportunity in earnings and consumption expenditure: the case of Indian men', *Review of Income and Wealth* 58(1): 679–706

Skocpol, T. and Williamson, V. 2012. *The Tea Party and the Remaking of Republican Conservatism.* Oxford and New York: Oxford University Press

Smelser, N. (ed.) 1988. *Handbook of Sociology.* Beverly Hills CA and London: Sage

Sorensen, A. B. 1996. 'The structural basis of social inequality', *American Journal of Sociology*, 101: 1333–65

Sorokin, P. 1927. *Social Mobility.* New York: Harper & Row

Standing, G. 2011. *The Precariat.* London: Bloomsbury

Statistics Sweden 2010. 'Inkomstfördelningsundersökningen 2008', www.scb.se

Statistics Sweden 2011. 'Befolkningen I Danderyd lever längst', press release 2011:72, www.scb.se

Statistics Sweden 2013a. 'Barn, föräldrar och separationer. Utvecklingen under 2000-.talet', *Demografiska rapporter* 2013(1), www.scb.se

Statistics Sweden 2013b. 'Kan yrket förklara skilsmässan?' www.scb.se

Statistics Sweden 2013c. 'Hushållens ekonomi', www.scb.se

Statistisk sentralbyrå 2012. 'Inntektsfordelningen, 1986–2011', www.ssb.no

Stiglitz, J. 2011 'Of the 1%, by the 1%, for the 1%', *Vanity Fair*, May

Stuckler, D., King, L. and McKee, M. 2009. 'Mass privatisation and the post-communist mortality crisis: a cross national analysis', *Lancet* 373(9661): 399–407

Sweezy, P. 1955. *The Present as History*. New York: Monthly Review Press

Tarkiainen, L., et al. 2011. 'Trends in life expectancy by income from 1988 to 2007: decomposition by age and cause of death', *Journal of Epidemiology and Community Health* 2010.123182

Tarkiainen, L., Martikainen, P. and Laaksonen, M. 2012. 'The changing relationship between income and mortality in Finland, 1988–2007', *Journal of Epidemiology and Community Health*, jech-2012-201097

Therborn, G. 1977. 'The rule of capital and the rise of democracy', *New Left Review* 103(May–June): 3–42

Therborn, G. 1984. 'The prospects of labour and the transformation of advanced capitalism', *New Left Review* 145: 5–38

Therborn, G. 1985. *Why Some Peoples Are More Unemployed than Others*. London: Verso

Therborn, G. 1995. *European Modernity and Beyond*. London: Sage

Therborn, G. 1996. 'Child politics: dimensions and perspectives', *Childhood* 1(3): 29–44

Therborn, G. 2004. *Between Sex and Power: Family in the World, 1900–2000*. London: Routledge

Therborn, G. (ed.) 2006. *Inequalities of the World*. London: Verso

Therborn, G. 2011. *The World: A Beginner's Guide*. Cambridge: Polity

Therborn, G. 2012a. 'Class in the 21st century', *New Left Review* 78: 5–29

Therborn, G. 2012b. 'Por qué en algunos países hay más paro que en otros? Parte II, 25 años más tarde' (Why some peoples are more unemployed than others. Part II, 25 years later)', pp. 227–52 in A. Guerra and J. F. Tezanos (eds.) *Alternativas económicas y sociales frente a la crisis*. Madrid: Editorial Sistema

Therborn, G. and Bekker, S. 2012. 'Conclusion', pp. 193–210 in S. Bekker and G. Therborn (eds.) *Capital Cities in Africa*. Cape Town: HSRC Press

Thomas, V., Yan Wang and Xibo Fan 2000. 'Measuring education inequality: Gini coefficient of education', World Bank Working Paper, www.worldbank.org

Thorat, S. and Newman, K. (eds.) 2010. *Blocked by Caste: Economic Discrimination in Modern India*. Oxford: Oxford University Press

Tilly, C. 1998. *Durable Inequality*. Berkeley and Los Angeles: University of California Press

Tocqueville, A. de. 1840/1961. *De la démocratie en Amérique*, 2 vols. Paris: Gallimard

Tocqueville, A. de 1856/1966. *The Ancien Régime & the French Revolution*. London: Collins/Fontana

Toye, R. 2010. *Churchill's Empire*. London: Macmillan

Tsutsui, J. 2010. 'The transitional phase of mate selection in East Asian countries', presentation at the ISA World Congress 2010, obtained from the author: junya_tsts@nifty.com

UN 2010. *The State of the World's Women*. New York: UN

UN Habitat 2008. 'State of the world's cities', www.unhabitat.org

UNDP 2005. *Arab Development Report 2005*. Geneva: UNDP

UNDP 2007. *Human Development Report 2007/8*, www.undp.org

UNDP 2011. *Human Development Report 2011*, www.undp.org

UNFPA 2011. 'Report of the global meeting on skewed sex ratios at birth', accessed on 19 July 2012, www.unfpa.org/home/publications/pubs/data

UNICEF 2004. *Innocenti Social Monitor 2004*. Florence: Innocenti Research Centre

UNICEF 2006. 'The state of the world's children 2006', www.unicef.org

UNICEF 2007. 'The state of the world's children 2007', www.unicef.org

UNICEF 2012. 'The state of the world's children 2012', www.unicef.org

Uslaner, E. 2002. *The Moral Foundations of Trust*. Cambridge: Cambridge University Press

Vågerö, D. 2006. 'Do health inequalities persist in the new global order? A European perspective', pp. 61–92 in G. Therborn (ed.) *Inequalities of the World*. London: Verso

Valkonen, T. 1998. 'Die Vergrösserung der sozioökonomischen Unterschiede in der Erwachsenenmortalität durch Status und deren Ursachen', *Zeitschrift für Bevölkerungswissenschaft* 23(3): 263–92

Varma, P. K. 1998. *The Great Indian Middle Class*. London: Viking

Volscho, T. and Kelly, N. 2012. 'The rise of the super-rich: power resources, taxes, financial markets, and the dynamics of the 1 per cent, 1949 to 2008', *American Sociological Review* 77(5): 679–99

WHO 2012. 'World Health statistics 2012', www.who.org

Wacquant, L. 2008. *Urban Outcasts*. Cambridge: Polity

Weisskopf, T. 2011 'Why worry about inequality in the booming Indian economy?' *Economic and Political Weekly* 46(47): 41–51

Westergaard, H. 1901. *Die Lehre von Mortalität und Morbidität*, 2nd edn. Jena

Wilkinson, R. 1996. *Unhealthy Societies*. London: Routledge

Wilkinson, R. 2005. *The Impact of Inequality*. London: Routledge

Wilkinson, R. and Pickett, K. 2009. *The Spirit Level*. London: Allen Lane

Wilson, W. J. 1987 *The Truly Disadvantaged*. Chicago: University of Chicago Press

Wolfe, B., Evans, W. and Seeman, T. (eds.) 2012. *The Biological Consequences of Socioeconomic Inequalities*. New York: Russell Sage Foundation

WLUML (Women Living Under Muslim Law) 2006. *Knowing Our Rights: Women, Family Laws and Customs in the Muslim World*, 3rd edn, accessed 20 July 2012, www.wluml.org/node/588

World Economic Forum 2012. 'Global competitiveness report 2012–13', www.worldeconomicforum.org

Wright, E. O. 1994. *Interrogating Inequality*. London: Verso

Wright, E. O. and Rogers, L. 2011. *American Society*. New York: W.W. Norton

Xu Anqi et al. 2007. 'Chinese family strength and resiliency', Digital Commons@University of Nebraska – Lincoln

Zang, Xiaowei 2008. 'Gender and ethnic variation in arranged marriages in a Chinese city', *Journal of Family Issues* 29(5): 615–38

Zhou Xiaohong 2008. 'Chinese middle class: reality or illusion?' pp. 110–26 in C. Jaffrelot and P. van der Veer (eds.) *Patterns of Middle Class Consumption in India and China.* New Delhi: Sage

Zhou Xiaohong and Qin Chen 2012. 'Globalization, social transformation, and construction of the Chinese middle classes', pp. 44–63 in Li Chunling (ed.) *The Rising Middle Classes of China.* Beijing and London: Social Sciences Academy Press and Paths International

Index